小经典译丛·民国名家名译

（汉英对照版）

# 幸福的摆

[德] R. 林道 等著　郁达夫 译

U0660086

辽宁人民出版社

# The Philosopher's Pendulum

by Rudolf Lindau et al
Translated by Yu Dafu

Ⓛ Liaoning People's Publishing House

**图书在版编目（CIP）数据**

幸福的摆：汉英对照 /（德）R.林道等著；郁达夫译. —沈阳：辽宁人民出版社，2017.1（2020.6重印）

（小经典译丛）

ISBN 978-7-205-08644-2

Ⅰ.①幸… Ⅱ.①R… ②郁… Ⅲ.①短篇小说—小说集—世界—汉、英 Ⅳ.①I14

中国版本图书馆CIP数据核字（2016）第166532号


出版发行　**辽宁人民出版社**

地址：沈阳市和平区十一纬路25号　邮编：110003

电话：024-23284321（邮　购）　024-23284324（发行部）

传真：024-23284191（发行部）　024-23284304（办公室）

http://www.lnpph.com.cn

印　　刷：**山东华立印务有限公司**

幅面尺寸：**110mm×180mm**

印　　张：**7**

字　　数：**95千字**

出版时间：**2017年1月第1版**

印刷时间：**2020年6月第2次印刷**

责任编辑：刘国阳

封面设计：展　志

版式设计：姿　兰

责任校对：耿　珺等

书　　号：ISBN 978-7-205-08644-2

定　　价：**23.00元**

# 目　录

# CONTENTS

# 幸福的摆

[德] R. 林道

## 一

多年的不见，海耳曼·法勃里修斯几乎把他们老友亨利·华伦忘记了。但是在大学里念书的时候，两人却是最要好也没有，曾经几次的设誓同盟，愿结为永久的朋友的哩。这是正当那一个时期里的事情，在这时期里青年是确信着"永久的友谊"的可能，而各自以为将来总有一番大业可成，或各自以为有一种天禀的奇才的，曾几何时，这一个时期也已成了过去，仿佛已经是去我们很远的样子。——现代的青年却聪明得多了。——可是当法勃里修斯和华伦的学生时代，两人都还幼稚得很，不但只在置酒高会的中间，两人欢饮着愿结为兄弟的誓酒，就是后来，在清醒的时候，也确信看他们将一生的如兄如弟，欢联过去，无论如何，总不会分离远隔的。

但是这一种无邪的狂热也只持续了不多时。等他们一长到成人，生活的铁手就将他们抓住，一个到东，一个到西，两人就被抛作了分飞的劳燕。——别离之后，几个月中间。他们原也曾常通详信，后来且也曾见过一次面的。可是两人终于暌隔了，信也渐渐儿地少了下去短了下去——终而至于闻问不通。对于一个朋友，虽感着满腔的热爱，但终日营营，竟没有工夫写十几行信的事情是常有的，一边对于能给人谋一点好事情的路人，我们却可以天天留下许多时候来招呼他。我们的如此，也是万不得已，于我们为人对友的诚挚正直，是毫没有关系的。——当这篇故事开场的时候，法勃里修斯已经记不清两人之间，究竟是哪一个写最后的一封信的，已经记不清，将从前的这样热心的通信切断者究竟是哪一个了。总之，两人间的书信已经断绝了许久，一年年地过去，从前是在面前活跃着的旧友的面貌，也一年年地消弱了下去模糊了下去，到最后几乎是完全忘记了的样子。——有几次，住在一个有大学校的都市里，在那里当教授，当著作家，曾博得了些相当的声誉的法勃里修斯，常常遇到一位学生，这学生分明是住在他的左近的。他头上有褐色的，卷曲的头发，脸上有一双喜乐勇敢，向世间直视的澄蓝的眼睛，年轻的嘴角更浮有一种和蔼可亲的微笑；一张白脸，不狡不伪，是真与信实的象征，使你可以信他，他也可以信你，在他眼睛里映射着的是莫名其妙的一种可以使你快乐的神情。法勃里修斯每遇到这一位青年，他总自然而然地会对自己说："十五年前，亨利的神气，也正是这一个样儿"——于是在几分钟间，他总要追思往昔，渴想和旧友华伦再谋一次见面的机缘。于这样的遇见着这青年之后，他也曾几次的发意，想对这一位行踪消失的友人的情状，去打听个明白；——可是屡次三番，这终不过是一个想头罢了。等回到了家中，他就有在桌上堆着的不得不阅读批评的新著，来催促原稿的出版所的书函，和要决定去否的招宴的请柬等看到——总之，日常的琐事，要马上裁决的事情，实在太多，在他能有工夫再想到华伦身上去之先，总已经是时间变得很迟，身心也已经在倦极的时候了。——在大多数人的生活里，时间总是这样地安排着，总只够做做必要的事情——或者以为是必要的事情——而已。

有一天午后，法勃里修斯和平时一样，到五点钟左右，走回家去的时候，听差的交给了他一封有美国邮印的来信。在未开封之前，他很注意地用了脑筋察看了一番。——封面上写地址的那种粗大不驯的字体，是很熟的，可是一时他却想不起来这究竟是谁人的笔迹。但忽然他脸上露出喜悦的形容来了："这是亨利的来信！"他叫着说。信内只写着短短的几行文字：

亲爱的海耳曼：

　　我们两人中间，至少是有一个人成名了，这是何等荣幸的事情。在一本书上，看见著者的名氏是你的时候，我就写了一封信去给那位替你出版的人，多谢他的好意，他立刻就写了封回信给我，因此我晓得了你的住址，现在能够告诉你了，我将于九月底回到故国的汉堡市来。请你写一封信到那里的邮局里存着给我，告诉我愿不愿我来和你聚晤几天。我于去故乡的途中，要从你现在住的那地方经过的，你若愿意和我相见，到时候我就可以下车来看你，在我是最喜欢也没有的事情。

你的老友亨利·华伦敬上

信后有一句附言——"这是现在的我"——法勃里修斯将一个附封的封袋打开来看，里头是一张相片。他拿了相片走近窗前，充满着沉痛的忧思，对此呆看了多时。相片上分明印着一位老人的面貌：虽则是很多很长，但已经是灰白的头发；一个阴郁的前额；深深凹进，有一种阴惨不安的目光凝视着的两眼；紧闭住的，有两条深纹锁着的那嘴角儿上，显然呈露着一种悲痛的形容。

"可怜的华伦！——他就变了这一个样子了么！——他比我还小一岁。还没有满三十六岁哩。"

法勃里修斯走到了镜子的前头，看了半天自己的相貌。当然，这面貌没有像他手里的相片上的面貌那么憔悴，虽然这也已经不是一个少年的相儿了，这也绝不是一个无忧无虑，乐天玩世的相儿。他的目光并不觉得阴惨迟钝，但也已经是衰弱倦怠了，嘴角儿上，和华伦的相片一样，也呈露着两条沉重的深纹。

"啊啊，两个人都已经老了，"法勃里修斯叹了一口气说，"我却有好久不曾想到这件事情上去过。"——于是他就坐了下来写信给他的朋友，告诉他说，自己因为两人不久可以相见，对这事情的喜悦正是没有言语可以形容。

第二天在街上，他却又遇见了那个常常使他想起华伦，有褐色的头发，和正直的喜笑的眼睛的青年。

"二十年后这一位青年大约也要变得和现在的我的那位老友一样的，"法勃里修斯自己对自己说，——"我们的生活，知道这玩意儿，能将活泼的眼睛弄成忧郁的，微笑的口嘴弄成皱纹很多的。——像我那么总算也还不坏，……虽然也说不上什么特别的好。自己总算平平地过去了半生；时常在这里感到一点满足，在那里又感到一点苦闷与忧心。我的青春就这样地消逝了，也不曾成就些特异的大业，也不曾遭遇到些什么。"

十月二日，法勃里修斯接到了一个从汉堡来

的电报，在这电报里华伦通告他说，他将于翌日午后的八点左右，到 L……市（莱比锡）来。到了时候，法勃里修斯为欢迎老友的到来，亲自去到火车站的前头。他看见他慢慢地，不能行动似的走下了车来，于走近他身边去之先，他又很仔细地审视了他一回，看究竟有没有认错。——他的这种衰老的样子，比相片上的更衰得多老得多了。穿的是一套灰色的行旅的衣服，在他的瘦而且长的身上，这套衣服飘飘然地松挂在那里。一顶阔边的帽子，这顶毡帽把他的额角和眼睛遮隐了。他向周围寻视了一回，似在寻找法勃里修斯的样子，然后慢慢地拖了疲倦的双脚走近了出口之处。法勃里修斯迎上去接他，华伦看见了他，一眼就认识了。一脸光明的，带有青年味的微笑在他的憔悴的脸上闪烁过了，很欢喜地，深深被感动地，他对他伸出了手来。

　　一个钟头之后，他俩坐在法勃里修斯的潇洒的屋里，在用俭约的晚饭了。华伦吃得很少。不过法勃里修斯却起初很惊异地，后来又不安地看出了一件事情来，就是这一位往年他当他做有节制的模范看的朋友，喝酒却过分地在喝。酒对他似乎是消失了醉人的效力的样子。他的苍白的脸上一点儿也不红起来，他的目光仍旧是冷冷的，在凝视似的，他的说话仍旧是很沉静，很缓慢，并不沉重起来。

侍食的使女，将杯盘收拾了去，把咖啡摆上桌子之后，走出房外去了。法勃里修斯安置了两张椅子，对他的朋友说：

"噢——现在我们只有两个人了。您且点上支雪茄抽口烟罢，在这张椅子上宽坐宽坐，将你在我们不会面的几年中间的事情讲给我听听。"

华伦推开了烟匣。

"你若不反对的话，"他说，"那我想将我的烟斗拿出来吸一筒淡巴菰。已经是习惯了，我觉得淡巴菰比最上等的雪茄味儿还要好些。"

说完他就从一只破旧的箱盒里抽了一支熏黑的，短短的木制烟斗出来。在这烟斗里他很有规则地将一种苍黑油润的淡巴菰装了进去。细心地点上了火，很响地啪啪吸了几口，吹出了几个大烟圈在面前的空气里后，他很明显地觉得满足似的说：

"一间很清静的房间——一位老友——食后

的一袋烟——并且又不必愁明日的生涯！啊，真好，真好！"

　　法勃里修斯从旁边打量了一回他这朋友，觉得有点奇怪起来了。这一位瘦而且长，头发灰白，眼睛暗淡无光，老在凝视似的人，这一位身体略向前屈，搁起腿儿，坐在自己的边上吸烟的人，哪里有一点像自己的少年朋友亨利·华伦？他是完全变了别一个自己所不认识的人了？法勃里修斯觉得有点奇怪，害怕起来了。——同时在他的心里又引起了一种深切的同情。使他变得这样，——把他的形状都换过了的他的身世，一定是如何的残酷，如何的悲惨呢。

　　"喂，"法勃里修斯把因使女的时时来往而打断的话头重新接起说，"您且说说看！——我们不会面的几年中间的事情。——或者您想先听我的自述么？"他很想将谈话弄得活泼一点，轻快一点，而在努力，但是他觉得，这努力终于不能够成功。

　　华伦尽在热心吸烟，不回答他。在这静默的中间法勃里修斯感觉起苦痛来了。他对于这一位他招待到自己屋里来的，很熟的，同时又觉得是别一个自己所不认识的客人，忽而感到了一种恐怖。最后他就鼓着勇气又说了一遍：

"喂，究竟你愿不愿意讲给我听，或者还是让我来先说罢？"

华伦轻轻地一笑。"我正在这儿想，"他说，"怎么回答你。——事实上，我却并没有什么可以讲给你听的。真奇怪得很，我自家想想看——这是我这一忽儿的默想的原因——我觉得在我的全生涯里并没有什么使我怀抱过苦闷。——你说我是多么蠢笨的一个傻子啊！说到这一个'并没有什么'——就是我的生涯——的享受，仿佛又是很不容易而且正因其如此仿佛又是十分有趣似的。总之我并不曾吃到十分的大苦。原是，我在无论什么地方也绝不曾有过什么的成功，可是我却也知道，在这一点我比成千成万的旁人也并不一定是更坏。烧烤好的鸽子当然没有飞到我的嘴里来，我也不曾得着过大白鸽票的头彩，我历来就辛辛苦苦只以勤劳去糊了半生的口，我也曾如一般人之所说，有过一次'不幸的恋爱'。——这是很久很久以前的事情——我早已安之若素了。这些事情现在早已不能够苦我。我这一忽儿觉得不平的，只是我的整个的生涯竟这样的没有欢乐，没有愉快地白白消失了去的一点。"

华伦停了一停，然后又慢慢地沉静地继续着说：

"没有几年前头，我还老在想着，事情或者会变一变过，或者会变得更好一点。我还正年轻哩，时运可实在不好。那时候我在纽约州的一个学堂里当薄俸的教员。在那里我将我能教的东西都担任了，凡我所知道的及因为要教所以同时不得不学的东西，如希腊文、拉丁文、德文、法文、数学、物理之类，并且在我的所谓闲空的时间里还有音乐。一天到晚，我简直没有一刻休息的工夫。一群闹得很厉害的，淘气的小孩子们包围着我，他们的唯一注意的工作，就是当我在教他们的时间中间，指摘我对他们所说的英语的错误。——到了晚上我就变得死也似的疲倦。——可是我在睡着之前，总有三四十分钟要开着眼睛做许多豪奢的梦。于是我就看见我自家处在一个幸福的、特异的境遇里：我得着了大白鸽票的头彩，烧烤好的鸽子突然会从空中的各方面飞到我的身边来，我变得很富有，很有名，很有势力……真是！……我使全世界，或者说爱伦·琪儿玛罢，因为她就是我的世界，惊异。——喂，海耳曼，你有没有和我一样的做过这些可笑的笨事情过？你有没有开了眼睛梦见过你自家已经成了内阁首相，百万富者，现代世上最大文学作品的著作人，得胜的元帅，议会里的政党首领或其他与此相类的人物？我是通通经验过了……当然是在梦里。——嗳，那真是最华美也没有的时代！

"我刚才说过的爱伦·琪儿玛，她是全校中最不喜欢读书的，一个我的学生的姊姊。可是这一个顽皮孩子的父亲，还在强硬地主张要他儿子学得些学问。于是在校里有大耐性之誉的我，就被选作对此事负责的人，当然报酬是很优的。因这一个机缘，我就被介绍到琪儿玛家屋里去了，又因为我偶然流露了些音乐的技能——你总大约还能记忆罢，除了专家之外，在平常的音乐爱好者中间，不是我弹钢琴弹得很好的么？——因此我就为教弗兰息斯以语学，教爱伦以音乐的原因，日日在琪儿玛家里进出了。

"老友，先请你把这环境想象一下，然后再

请你笑我的痴愚，和我自家已经千遍万遍地笑过自家一样。你瞧，对手方面呢，——就是琪儿玛家的一方面呢，——有千万的巨富和与此不相下的自负骄矜。一位很狡猾而伶俐的父亲，一个虚荣心很大而最喜夸饰的母亲，一个他们一家的希望所钟的顽皮淘气的儿子，一个如花美丽，很有教养，举止娴雅，而且是理性丰富的十九岁的女儿。——还有一方面呢，是二十九岁的博士亨利·华伦先生。——在梦里呢，他是一个划时代的哲学著作的著者，或者北军的得胜将军，或者联邦共和国的大总统，虽然照美国的法例，大总统必须是在美国出生者方有资格，而亨利是在查儿河上的泰儿培出生的；——在实际上呢，他是一个七十块金洋一月的爱儿米拉高中的教员。——大约你总相信罢？我最初对于自家的这没有希望的癞虾蟆想吃天鹅肉的身份的可笑，是知道的这一件事情，你总相信罢？——当然我是明了的。我在不做梦的时候，也是一个很有理性的人，读书读得很多，自知也很明白，绝不会失进退之度的，我又不是疯了，哪里会想我自家有和爱伦结婚的可能的呢？我很明白确实地知道，这事情的不可能，和我的不能够做美国联邦共和国的大总统一样。——可是呵，我还是在那里做梦，在那里痴想和这位百万豪富的女儿结婚，——话可又要说回来了，对我自己公平地判断起来，觉得我个人的这情热，并不是对一个什么人有什么妨害的。将此情热在我的脑中蓄养，在我是一种秘密的，无邪的享乐。关于这事情，我也绝不想对人说出来，如关于我的梦想我自己做了朴督马克的总司令等一样。但是聪明的爱伦，对于我这缄默的，秘密的爱情，似乎有些看出来了。虽然她并没有片言只语，或一眼眼色流露出来表示她的晓得我对她的状态，可是我却毫无疑念地确信着她看出了我的隐衷。她的这种谨严不露声色的态度，只有一件小小的偶然的事情，对它反叛破露了一次。

"有一天我看见她眼睛哭得很红肿。我当然不敢去问她，是什么苦得她如此。她当听讲的当中，也是十分错乱不注意的样子。我教完了正想走的时候，她却把眼毛低下，眼睛审视着地面对我说：'我，我恐怕这学课不得不休止些时候了。这在我是很怅恨的。我只，只祝望你的好，华伦先生。'——说完她对我看也不看一眼就很急速地走出房外去了。我如同听到了一个晴天的霹雳。这几句话,她讲话的那一种凄楚的音调,究竟是什么意思呢?到了第二天,弗兰息斯来传达他爸爸的客气话后,告诉我说,他也要得四天的休假,在这四天之内我可以不必到他家里去,因为他姊姊和一位纽约的富商霍华德先生订婚,屋里将要设盛大的宴会的缘故。——到此我所猜不透的哑谜方才被他说破,而我到此时为止把我的生活甜蜜化的梦想也告终结了。

"根本地说起来,爱伦的结婚与否,和林肯去后约翰生的继他而被选为美国总统等事情一样,对我是并没有什么不幸之可言。她的出嫁,美国总统的更换等,以理性说起来,于我有什么丝毫的关系呢?可是,朋友,你却想不到这一件事情——我说的是这一次的婚约——对我是如何的一个大打击呀。我的全部的'一无所有'忽然显示在我的面前。我的空中楼阁都倒毁了下来。我终于看到了在实世间的我自己:一个学校的教师——既没有过去的功业著作可以夸示于人,在现在也没有一点人生的乐趣,对将来呢,更是一点儿希望也没有了。"

　　在讲话的中间，他的烟斗已经熄了。华伦很仔细地把烟斗里的残烬清了出来。于是他就从袋里拿出了一块用果汁制过的甜味板烟来，用小刀切下了正足装一筒用的烟丝之后，他就装进了烟斗，点上了火又重新很舒服地在吸了。在这样装点的中间，他并不说话，只轻轻地在齿间吹了几声口笛。法勃里修斯也同样地不作一声。停了一忽，很快很重地抽了几口之后，烟斗里啾地烧得很旺了，华伦又继续说：

　　"我在一个相当的时期内觉得非常的懊丧。并不是因为失掉了爱伦——因为一个从没有得到过什么，绝没有得到的权利的人，是不会感到失掉的——却因为我自己的那一种幻象的消失。我吃尽了无数的自知之树的果实，尝尽这些果实的无限的苦味。——我离开了爱儿米拉，到别处去寻我的幸福。我对于我自己的职业问题是很有把握的，并且从实地的经验上我也知道如何能得到最高的薪俸。我在职业上从没有过失业的事情，渐渐地一处一处我在美国的六七州里飘泊着教书也得到了相当的成功。我现在已经记不清了，曾在哪些地方教过书，在萨克拉门多，在芝加哥，在圣路易，在新西奈底，在波士顿，纽约……各道各处——各道各处。我无论在什么地方总只见到一样的淘气的，偷懒的学生和一样的希腊拉丁文里的规则和不规则动词。假如你想见到一个对学生及古典语文法完全厌倦了的人的时候，那你只看我就对了。

　　"在无聊闲空的时间里——虽则我做的事情很多，但我却总有这些闲空无聊的时间的——我就把我浑身的注意力投入到了哲学问题的思考里去。我的抽烟抽得很多的习惯，就是在这些时间里养成的呀……"他忽而停住不说了，仿佛是在追思什么的样子，双眼呆呆地只在向空中凝视。然后用了他那只瘦骨棱棱的手向额上的头发掠了一掠，又慢慢地茫然自失似的重复着说："嗳，抽烟抽得很多……我还得了些另外的习惯，"他又比较快一点继续着说，"但是这些和我所说的故事却无关系的。"

　　"将我的时间的大部分占去的，是一个我所发明的所谓'幸福的摆'的摆动原理。从这一个原理里我得到了安稳的觉悟，幸赖着此我一时方得安身立命，而今天你才得见到我这一副心平气和的样子。我常常自慰着说，我的大大的不幸——假如许我将我的心境没有客气地这样命名的说话——是从我自己的过分的奢望，希望着过分的幸福，而来的。——假如一个人在梦里将自己抬得这样高，变成了一个世界有名的人物，变成了爱伦·琪儿玛的男人，那醒来的时候于双脚得再踏实地之先，不得不深深地跌坠是应该的，这并不是一件奇事。假如我在我的希望里更安分谦抑一点，那这希望的实现当然要更容易，而最坏的幻灭，至少也更要减少一点苦味。——从这一个据最近的经验看来是明确的根本原理讲起来，我可以得到一个像底下那么的论理的结论，就是在人力所能做到的范围以内，想避去不幸的最上法门，是竭力的不要去希望幸福。这原是耶稣降生以前几世纪的先哲们所发现的真理，我也不想把这古代的思想据为己有而要求发明特许之权。可是将这真理表示出来的一个征象，至少我相信是我的发明。"

"请你给我一张纸和一支铅笔，"他朝向坐在边上的法勃里修斯继续着说，"我只需画它几笔就能够将这原理表示得非常简单明白。"

　　法勃里修斯不说一句话，将他朋友所要求的纸笔递给他。——华伦在纸上画了一个大大的，向上开的半圆圈，在这半圆中间画了一个向下垂直的摆，这摆的下端，正与半圆的底点相触，在时钟的圆面上，这正是Ⅵ字的地方。向右手的边上，自下面画起，在时钟的Ⅴ，Ⅳ，Ⅲ字等地方，他各写了这几个字："守分的愿望"——"热情的希求，功名心"——"对幸福的过分的渴想，夸大狂"。——将纸又移回来，向摆的左手，自下而上，在时钟面的Ⅶ，Ⅷ，Ⅸ等字的地方，他又写了"怨恨和不平"——"苦恼，痛苦的幻灭"——"绝望"几个字。最后在摆的下面正是Ⅵ字的地方底下，他画上了一个圆圆的粗点。他一面很自在地微笑着，一面又在细心地用铅笔在这一点里画上阴影去。在这一个底点的下面，他写了这几个字："死点。完全的静止"。

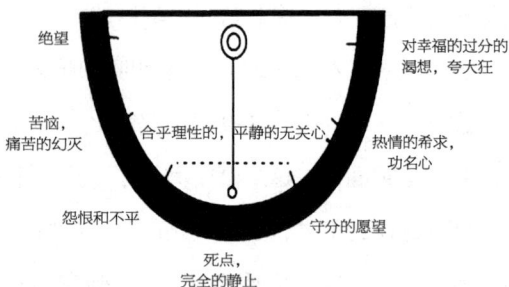

他然后把头歪在一边，眉毛蹙得高高，仿佛是要吹口笛似的，把嘴尖起，很注意地将这图看了半分钟于是他又说："这罗盘针还没有完全在'死点'和右边的'守分的愿望'与左边的'怨恨和不平'之间，是属于一条美丽的'合乎理性的，平静的无关心'线的……但是这图，即使像现在的样子，已尽够阐明我的定理了。——你信从我的意见么？"

法勃里修斯只沉默着点了点头。一种深沉的哀思，已经笼罩上他的心身了。他又举起眼睛来凝视了一回他的这位少年时候的挚友。对这位挚友，他从前是曾经祝望他有一个伟大的将来的，就是现在，法勃里修斯也还只在祝望他的好的，而他却变成了一个可怜的偏执狂者了。

"你瞧，"华伦很沉静地继续着说，仿佛他是在向一群注意听讲的学生们讲科学讲义似的，"假如我现在轻轻地将这幸福的摆向右手举起，正举得触着'守分的愿望'之点那么高，然后就撒手放下，那这摆当然只会走回向'怨恨和不平'之点，这一点它再也不会越过的。它将在这两点之间的'合乎理性的，平静的无关心'线上摆动些时，最多也不过摇动一生的时间，然后终将止于'死点'而变成'完全的静止'。——这实在是安慰我们，使我们心平气和的一个想头！"——他静止了一忽儿，像在等法勃里修斯的反驳似的。可是法勃里修斯只呆呆地沉默着没有说话，所以他又继续说：

"你大约现在总已经了解了罢，我底下所想说的结论。假如我将这摆举起，举到'热情的希求'或'夸大狂'等点的时候，那它一定会摇回到'苦恼'或'绝望'上去的。这事情是明显得很的，是不是？"

"是的，明显得很的。"法勃里修斯只悄然地沉郁地回答了一声。

"是呵，"华伦热心地继续着说，"可惜我把它发现得太迟了。如我已经和你讲过的一样，我在梦里所想的事情，实在是非同小可。我想做共和国的大总统，打胜仗的元帅，世界有名的学者，爱伦的丈夫。——哼！——一个应该安分的人哪。——你说怎么样？——我和妄想狂者似的把那幸福的摆举得太高了，所以它突然地从我这双无力的手里滑落的时候，就飞打了过去，不得不摇半个大圈而回到'绝望'的地方去了。——那真是些艰险，苦痛的时间呵！——我希望你没有这样的苦过，如那时候的我一样。——我真如同在一个噩梦里做着人的样子……真如同在一种最难过的恶醉里……"他的言语又同先前一样窒塞住了。忽而他又狂暴地高笑了起来……"呵呵！真如同在一种恶醉里！——我就拼命地喝起酒来了……"他的因狂笑的痉挛抽缩得阴险怕人的颜面到此又突然变得很认真而高雅，并且全身战栗着说："一个人当有自觉地沉沦下去的时候，实在是一件可怕的事情。"——他沉默了好久，然后又重新把他的烟斗装满，移转身体向着法勃里修斯问说：

"关于我一生的事情，你已经听够了没有？或者你还想听听这一段故事的结局罢？"

　　法勃里修斯又悄然地回答他说："听你这样的讲，实在使我伤心，但是请，请你说下去罢，或者说完了倒反好些。"

　　"是的，把我心里的郁积倾吐一次，或者是要好些……所以我就吃上了酒……这一种轻贱的自暴自弃的习惯，在美国是很容易染成的……有几处地方，我就为此而不得不抛去我的位置，因为他们觉得我的品行已经是不复可敬了。可是寻一个新的位置，是一点儿也不费力的。我从来没有感到过经济上的穷迫，虽然我的生活也并不是过于富裕。我所要花的钱本来是不多。到此我衣饰也不讲究了。书也不再买了。——离开爱儿米拉的一年半之后，有一天，在纽约的中央公园里我忽而撞见了爱伦。她结婚之后，已经有十五个月了。这是我晓得的。她一见我就认识了，来招呼我，和我说话。那时候我真想往地底里钻下去。我晓得我的衣冠是褴褛得不堪，样子是很潦倒的。我心里相信，我的甘心自愿的堕落，她一定已在我的脸上看穿了。但是她并不说一句话，或者她是不愿意说。她伸出手来给我，并且用了她那种柔和的声气对我说：

"'我真喜欢得很，我们终究又遇见了。我曾经问过父亲，问过弗兰息斯以你的事情；但他们都不晓得你在什么地方。我十分诚恳地请求你，请你在这一个冬天再来教我些音乐。你晓得我的住址罢——'她就把她的住址给我。

"我对她这些和蔼的话，只嗫嚅地做了几声惑乱的回答。她很情深地微笑着朝我看看，忽而又变得很诚挚地同情似的问我说：

"'你莫非病了么？我觉得你仿佛是很憔悴的样子。'

"'是，是的，'我回答说，心里很欢喜，因为我却找到了一个可以遮掩我的潦倒的外观的口实了。'我是病了，现在还没有复原哩。'

"'这这真使我难过，'她轻轻地说。——法勃里修斯，请你轻笑我！请你痛骂我这不可救度的愚人！可是我可以赌着咒告诉你，在她的眼睛里我的确看出了些超出乎平常一般的，虚文的同情以外的东西来。这一种为我愁虑，对我怜惜的柔情，在她的眼光里闪耀着。我觉得全身被一种不可言说的苦痛紧扎住了。啊啊，我究竟造了些什么孽，要受苦到这一步田地呢？痛饮，不安，失眠的夜晚等竟把我弄得成了一个毫无自持力的病弱者了。我跟跄倒退了一步，感乱地注视着她。这中间大都会的繁殷的生息正和潮水似的在我们的周围汹涌着哩。

"'你马上来看我，你一定马上来看我，'这样很快地说着，她就不由自主地走开去了。我看见她走进了一乘车子，她分明是从这车子里出来到公园来散步的。我注视着她，又看见她那张灰白的颜面伏出在车窗外头，当她临去经过我身边的时候，还在车窗外对我用了惊愕，凝视的眼光在呆看。

"我走回家来。我的回家的路线是要经过她的住处的。她住在一所宫殿似的大洋楼里。我闷坐在一间可怜的客舍的小房间里又做起梦来了：爱伦是爱我的，她是在叹美我崇拜我的，我还没有把她失掉哩。那个摆又高高指上疯狂的期待上去了。

"老友，你若能够的话，那请你解释给我听，这究竟是怎么一回事？一个很有理性，很沉静的人，——因为我在日常生活里总是很沉默，很有理性的；就是在离开他们以后的今日，而那些八

年间我曾经寄住在他们中间，正直勤劳以教授希
腊拉丁文而糊过口的各学校委员们的眼里，我也
还是一个沉静而有理性的人，——请你解释给我
听，这究竟是怎么的，就是像这样的一个沉静
有理性的人，有时候虽明明自家知道，可是终
于会完全变成一个疯子的，这究竟是怎么一回
事？——你的说明，也可以说是我的辩解，我极
愿意承认，这一种状态确是一种神经病的预兆，
其后我就为这病所缠住，不得不在病床上卧睡了
许多个礼拜。

　　"病渐恢复的中间，我又变得很沉静而有理
性，可是我的青春的生命也就此完结了。在两个
月的时日之内我竟老了二十岁的年纪。我离开
病房的时候，就变得衰老龙钟，像现在的样子
了。我的过去，虽则是这样空虚而乏味的，却成
了我的生涯的全部。现在我已经没有什么事情可
以做，没有什么可以希望，没有什么可以渴想的
了。已经是黄昏的世界了，熙扰和火热的白昼已
经过去了，境地变得凉爽清平。那个摆只是懒懒
地在一个短小的距离内在那条'合乎理性的，平
静的无关心'线上摇动了……我却真想知道知

道，那些在世上成就功名，达到他们的目的的人，那些真的成了得胜的元帅，内阁的首相，和其他与此相类的伟人的人，心状究竟是怎么样的。不晓得他们在人生的晚境，究竟能否感到一种得意的满足而休止，不晓得他们是否也只感到一种奋斗的疲倦而并没有胜利的喜悦，也只懒懒地退出那人生的漩涡。——难道无论哪一个人，为幸福这一个刑罚所禁止，就不能下降到他的内部深处，去算清他的以消耗生命而换得的东西的么？"

华伦静默了好久，只沉浸在痛苦的沉思里。然后他又轻轻地继续着说：

"我对于爱伦的招请，当然，没有应她。但是她不知从哪里寻得了我的住处，并且也知道了我的害病。——这可并不是一幕浪漫的恋爱情景。我的床前，并没有她的辉耀的倩影前来看病，我在我的发热的乱梦里，也没有觉得她的冰冷的素手按上我的火热的额头上来。我只在病院里调养，并且他们也看护得我很好，我在那里叫作第三百八十二号，而这冗长的故事全部，也只是一件疏散无味的东西。——可是到了我想脱离病院

对那慈和的院长诀别的时候，他却交给了我一封
信和五百元金洋的一张支票。在那个封筒里有像
底下那么的一张信：

　　你的一位老朋友，请求你将封入的金额
接受，当作他借给你的款子，等你病好之后找
到了工作，再每月地还他，每月付到这病院
里来。

　　"——这信是不署名的！

　　"这事情明明是对我的好意；可是却也使我
痛心得很。我当然不得不辞却这金钱的惠借。假
使我让一位我所热爱过而终与他人结婚的女人来
帮助我，那也就是大大的过失。

　　"我就问那个当我在读信的中间很得意地笑
着在旁边观察我的院长，问他晓得不晓得，这发
信人是谁。他回答我说不晓得。但是我却明明知
道，他是在对我保守着秘密。——我想了一忽儿，
然后又重新问他，问他能不能替我转送一封信给
这位写信给我的人。这一件事情他答应了。于是
我就对他说，明天可以将那信交给他的。

"我想了半天，想这封信将如何的写法。一边我在心里却一点儿也没有疑念，知道这将钱送给我的一定是爱伦。对此好意我却不愿意有所辜负，我真不愿意伤坏她的感情。可是我终于写定了一封信，现在就我的记忆所及，大约这信的内容是如此的：

我真感谢你得很，但是你借给我的钱，我却不能够收受。请你心里不要难过，因为我将钱送还了给你。你的为此，明明是为了我的好。以后我将努力的为人，使我不至于辜负你这一种深情。请你相信我，在我心上将永远保留着你的记忆。你的好意我是没齿也不能忘记的。

"将这信交给病院院长之后没有几天，我就离开了纽约到了美国西岸的散弗兰西斯珂。——往后好几年我没有见到听到爱伦·琪儿玛的事情。她的印象也渐渐地消弱了下去。我已经把她忘了。我并且也忘记了我是曾经有过年轻的时代的。我是老了。——那条暗淡的河流，将载着我和我的幸福的小舟并无激动很和平地流送到那个最后是无人不去的神秘的海里去的那条暗淡的河流，不过在一个荒凉的大漠里经过了它的流程。我所航过的河流两岸，只是惨淡怖人的单调罢了。我是，啊啊，极端厌倦地站在这扁舟的——人生的舷上。——我从没有故意地做过恶事。美的物事我是爱的，善的事情我是想勉力做的。——为什么我会这样地感不出人生的乐趣来的呢？我对于可以冲破我这只船底的岩石，对于能将我卷入河流深处去的涡漩，倒反想祝福它们。——到我听见爱伦的婚约那一日止，我还老是相信，我的生活将于明日重新开始。这一个明日到了，可是我的新生活仍没有开始——而我的生涯已经是完结了。"

华伦现在说话说得这样地轻，弄得法勃里修斯要听他的话的时候不得不耸肩努一番力了。与其说他是在和他的朋友说话，倒反不如说他在和自己说话更像些。他将右手的食指高高举起，指示着一个摆的摇动，从右到左地在空中慢慢画了半个短圈。然后将手指指上那个在纸上他所画过的黑点，轻轻地说："完全的静止……我只希望，各事都快点过去。"

　　一个长时间的静默继续了下去，终至法勃里修斯因难耐而破了这个沉默。

　　"那你又怎么，"他问说，"决心离开美国，回到欧洲来的呢？"

　　"是的，不错，"华伦忽而同惊醒似的回答说，"还少个所谓结尾罢。本来我这故事就没有结局的……和它的也没有冒头是一样。这故事所述的不过是些无形状的，无目的的事情罢了；并不是人的一生，却只是人的丧生——死。——但是你若还没有疲倦的话，那我还可以依了年代的顺序继续说下去。"

　　"请你继续说下去。"

　　"是的……我在美国各处流浪了好几年。那个幸福的摆是很有规则地限制住了。它只在很容易达到的'守分的愿望'和不再长时苦我的'怨恨和不平'之间摆动。——我开始了一种安静的简易生活，人家都把我当作一个怪人看了。我只勤勉忠实地做完我的义务责任，旁人的事情一点儿也不去闻问了。一到了我的钟头教完闲空下来的时候，我就一个人走出市外到最近的树林里去休卧在大树之下。一年四季的时间，在我是一样的；养花的春季，丰殷浓绿的夏天，悲哀的秋日，荒冷的冬时，在我都是一样的好的。我总只觉得树林的可爱。静默的树林我觉得是世界上最美的东西。在树林里有一脉和平之气会吹入到我的心里来的。我变得非常的和平安静了，对于在我周围的事事物物毫不关心，甚至于成了这样的一种习惯，变得凡对关于我的无论何物，和对向我提议或劝止的无论何事，我都只回答一个'很好很好'。我自己却毫不曾注意到这一个回答，这一个字是非常自然地流到我的口头上来的，到了有一天一位同事对我说，在校里人家给我取了一个绰号叫'很好很好先生'，我才觉得。——人人对我这么一个从来也不曾遇到过好事情的人，叫我'很好很好'，岂不是一件很滑稽的事情么？

"现在我只需告诉你一段最后的小小的冒险，我的故事就可以算完结，希望来听你的了。

"去年我偶尔到了爱儿米拉，是学校里休假的期中。我没有什么事情好做，口袋里还存着几百块的金洋钱在那里。我决心再去看一遍我那悲喜交感过的背景故地。自我离开那里之后已经有七年了。我十分有把握，确信着在那里再也没有一个人能认识我了，并且即使被他们认出了，在我也更有什么要紧？

"当我在市上走了一圈之后，看访了一回我曾在教书过的学校和爱伦·琪儿玛住过的邸宅以后，我就走上那个市外的小公园去，在这公园里当我年轻的当日，曾经消磨去许多幻想的时间，并且那园里的一草一木，我当时也都认识的。那些我在那里的时候都还是矮矮的小树，现在已经长成了摩天的大木了。树木中长成大树的也不是全部。这里那里有几株是枯死了的，有几株是被砍伐了的。——那是新秋的九月——将晚的时候。太阳已沉落在西天，红红的炫目的夕照阳光，穿过了苍黑的树枝在那里闪射。——在一棵树下的椅子上，有一个暗黑的人影坐在那里。无情无绪地走近了那黑影的身边，我真吃了一惊，我马上就认清了。——她是爱伦，——我被钉钉住似的立住了一忽儿。

"她身体屈俯向前坐着，在用了遮日光的伞子长柄向地上的泥沙里画字。——她穿的是一身丧服——她还没有看见我哩。我屏住了气不声不响地仍复离开了她。走远了百数步后，我从那条树荫下的甬道里走入了旁边树木的底下，在树下我又惊惶地回转来看了一眼。她还是仍旧坐在那里。啊啊，只有上帝知道，何以这一种想头会突然又涌到我的脑里来的。我想看她一看了。她已经是不会认识我的这事情，我是确实知道的。我于是装作在散步的一位闲人的样子慢慢走近了她的身边，几分钟后，我就走到了她的前头了。——她在路上看见了我的黑影，毫不注意地将她的头儿举起，我们的四条视线就冲接在一道。我的心脏的鼓动仿佛要停止的样子。她的目光是不相关的，冷冷的。可是一忽儿的中间，她眼睛里突然放起异样的光来了，她把身体急速地掣动了一下，似乎是要站起来似的。此外我不能看见了。我已经走过了她的身边，一步一步地离她远了，绝对不敢转过头来，再回看她一眼。我还没有走到公园出口处之前，一辆无篷的敞车很快地在我的身边转过；我又看见了爱伦，看见她靠出在车外，脸色苍白，眼睛张得很大，同五年前头在纽约的中央公园外看见她的时候一样。——我为什么不同她招呼呢？——真是愚人愚事，——但我终没有招呼她。她那双眼睛，约有一分钟的时间，忧心似的向我注视着的她那双眼睛，忽而又变得冷冷的了。我还看见她深深地吐了一口气，然后又慢慢地将身体靠回了车中。——然后她就去我远了，消失了。

"我现在是三十六岁了。可是还不免有点羞缩，当我将我所做的那件应该是小学生才配做的愚事在此地不得不对你说出的时候。我写了一封信给她：'一个十分尊敬你的朋友，对于他，你在数年前曾经示以好意的，他昨天也曾见过你一面，可是你不曾认出他来，他在这里送上他的一个敬礼。'——这信当我在乘上自爱儿米拉开向纽约去的火车一分钟前投在邮筒里的，那时候我的心脏鼓动得非常厉害，仿佛是正在冒险做一件极危险的事情似的——这真是一个大冒险呵！是不是？……我平生觉得从没有经验过比这事情更大的冒险，就是现在，在我的回忆里，我也常常只以此而在自慰的哩！

"差不多过了一年之后，在去今没有几个月以前，我偶尔在百老汇路上又撞见了今年是长到

了二十岁的弗兰息斯·琪儿玛。——世界实在是
小不过——认识的人是怎么也会撞见的。——
长得和他姊姊很像的弗兰息斯，已经不认识我
了——是我招呼他的。他很和气而又很困惑地微
笑着朝我看了几分钟。——忽然他就满心欢喜地
向我伸出了手来。

　　"'啊，华伦先生！'他叫着说，'我真喜欢，
终于又见到你了！我和爱伦常在谈起你，并且猜
想你不知究竟怎么样了。——你为什么一点儿也
不使我们知道一点消息呢？'

　　"我回答说，'这些没有价值的事情，我怕敢
使你们知道。'我说话说得非常之幽。现在我是
很有勇气了。但在当时那青年却使我变得胆怯。
可是我却从来没有向他要求过什么，也不再期望
他些什么的哩。

　　"弗兰息斯以青年的和蔼的热忱回答说：

　　"'对我们这样的狐疑，那是你的不是。你是
我的唯一的先生，只有从你那里我才学得了些物
事，我衷心所感谢的，只有你一位先生。你想我
会把我们的那些长时间的，美丽的散步忘记的
么？那时候我虽则还是一个小孩子，可是在那时

候你讲给我听的一切善的美的事情，都还牢牢铭刻在我的记忆里哩。——爱伦吗？——她自先生你去后，就不愿意再学音乐，她现在在那里弹奏的，还只是从你那里学来的那些老调子，她不愿意再学些另外的音乐。'

'父亲母亲都好么？——你姊姊怎么样了？'我问。

'可怜的母亲三年前病故了，'弗兰息斯回答说。'现在在我们家里管理家务的是爱伦。'

'那么你们姊夫也和你们一道住的么？'

'姊夫？'弗兰息斯很怪异地回答。'难道你还不晓得么？去年他坐船从里凡浦儿到纽约来的途中，那只"阿脱兰脱"号沉没了。'

"我一句话也说不出来。

"'是的，'弗兰息斯直率平静地追加上去说：'这是不能够向外人说的；他的死也算不得一个大损失。姊夫并不是一个好人。在他突然遭难之先，爱伦已经和他离开别居了三年了。——他俩的结婚生活，并不是幸福的。'

"我把头动了一动，做了一个表示我的同感的姿势。但是无论如何，却总不能够说出一句话来。

"'你一定马上就来看我们，'弗兰息斯继续着说，'此地是我的卡片。——请你决定一个日子，到我们家里来吃饭。我们一家都在希望着见你哩！'

"我回答他说：我将写信给他，我们就此分别了。

"我的精神——我想，幸亏是如此——已经将它的少年时候的弹性消失尽了。那个摆这一回并不高举起来。它只在数年来来往摆动惯的那个短距离的小弓形内摇动。我自己晓得，和琪儿玛家一族的重新的关系一定又要发生苦痛和失望的。我觉得我自己还没有完全的把握，一到爱伦的面前，我怕自家又要变成一个呆子的。我有十足的理性，足够看出向这位富有的，高贵的，年轻的寡妇求婚是一种疯狂。同时我又觉得，只须短短的和爱伦在一道几天，我这可怜的理性又会完全失掉的。——我在各抒情诗里也曾读过，知道爱情能使人净化，能使他变而为神。——可是爱情也能使他变为顽迷的傻子。这至少在我这一回的事里是如此的，所以我不得不加意地留心。

　　"在我和弗兰息斯·琪儿玛遇见的前几天，我曾接到有一位我的旧亲死去的通知。——关于他的记忆，我已经有点记不大清楚了。——我只记得小孩子的时候，曾在他那里住过一个假期，那时候他待我是很亲热的。他是一位沉静而率真的人，只寂寥地过了他的一生。我模糊地记得曾听见人说过，他从前是对我母亲发生过爱情的，等她结婚之后，他就避去了尘世，在乡间过他的孤独生活了。有许多年不曾听到他的事情了。可是现在推想起来，这一位悲哀沉郁的老人，仿佛是把我常放在心里，从没有把我忘记过似的。总之，他在临终之前，曾把他的小小的财产的大部分赠遗给了我。因此我就变了一间在附近的很安适的房子的所有者，和一块永年出租的不动产的主人了。每年的一千二百'泰来'的租金，已经尽够我全部的开销了。

　　"于是我就决心马上离开美国，回到我的多年不见的故乡里来。你的住址，我已经打听到了。我在想，和你，我的最旧的唯一的老友的相见之欢，一定能将我在一生中所受的苦痛减轻几分。我到这里来一看，觉得这推想果然没有错。

我终于有了这一次——还是第一次哩——将我胸中的苦闷尽情吐露的机会，我现在觉得心里轻快得多了，这是我年来所没有感到过的事情。——我晓得你不会责备我过于严苛。——你一定在伤痛我的软弱，但我晓得你不会因此而下一个严苛的判断。——我平生原没有做过一件好事——但也没有犯过一件坏事。我是一个完全无用的东西，同《杜葛纳夫》（*Turgenev*）那篇阴惨的小说里的一位悲哀的主人公一样，是一个零余者。

　　"我在从纽约出发之先，曾写了一封信给弗兰息斯·琪儿玛。——我告诉他，一位亲戚的突然的死亡，使我不得不回到欧洲来。我把你的通信地址给他，可以使他不至于看出我在逃避和他们一家的来往交际，以后我就出发了。现在我却在此地了。——好，总算讲完。Dixi！"

　　在讲话的中间，没有使他的烟斗熄灭过的华伦，马上要求他的朋友法勃里修斯，也将他自己的历史讲出来给他听。可是法勃里修斯却已觉得伤心之至，在消沉的情绪里不想再说话了。所以他就告诉他的朋友，时间已经晚了，并且提议说，明天再来将这谈话继续下去。华伦回答说：

"很好很好。"将烟斗里的烟煤敲出，他就把还在桌上放着的一瓶酒拿起，把瓶里残余的酒和法勃里修斯两人分倒了。然后他将杯举起，很快乐地叫着说："为纪念我俩的青春！"——连杯里的最后一滴也吞饮尽了以后，他将杯子放回桌上，感到很满足似的说：

"这是我年来干饮过的第一杯适口的酒。因为我今天所饮的，并不是为了想忘记过去，而是为了纪念着过去。"

## 二

华伦在他的朋友法勃里修斯那里住了好几天。法勃里修斯觉得他朋友是他生平遇到过的人中间的一个最质朴最谦逊的人。他对什么东西都不再要求，无论什么你给他，他总是觉得满足的。法勃里修斯对他提议无论什么事情，他的回答总只是"很好很好"——假如法勃里修斯有时候不去和他说话呢，他却会自得其乐于在安乐椅里坐着抽烟，手里或拿一本书，可是他并不是读得很起劲的，他从他那短烟斗里向空中吹吹一个个大的烟圈，就似乎是与世与人都无争恨似的和平适意。——他说，他很不喜欢会见生人。可是时常在法勃里修斯家里进出的几个人，和他也算结了表面上的相识的几个人，都觉得他是一位很有学问很谦和的长者。凡接近他的人，总没有一个是不喜欢他的。他身上有一种特异的足以使人欢喜的牵引力。法勃里修斯也觉不能了解，华伦的这一种特质究在什么地方，可是他自己也不能逃出华伦的这一种迷力的影响。他在几日中间，又对华伦有起那种同在少年的学生时代一样的献身的亲密的友谊来了——"谁能禁得住不爱他呢。"法勃里修斯每自己对自己说。"爱伦·琪儿玛的爱他，也决不是一件奇事，是应该的，……我真想尽我的能力，来把他弄得快乐一点。"

有一天晚上法勃里修斯带了他的朋友到一家戏园里去，在那里有一出滑稽的短剧是演得很好的。他记得华伦做学生的时代对于这一类的东西是特别喜欢，在这一种剧场里他是最快乐也没有的。当时他朋友的那一种快乐的，清新的笑声，还在法勃里修斯的耳朵里响着哩。——但是到了那里法勃里修斯又感到了一种新的失望。——华伦一点儿也没有兴趣地在那里看这一出滑稽短剧。旁边在静静地观察他的法勃里修斯看他一次也没有笑过。他不过很注意地听了一刻，可是歇了一歇，他就把这一个视听的注意抛去，似乎是不愿再去用心看取的样子，只在无精打采地看戏园的周围了。到了第二幕完结，法勃里修斯问他"我们还是回去呢还是怎么"的时候，他很快地回答说："很好很好，我们回去罢！对这一种没意思的滑稽我已经感不到趣味了。还是让我们去抽一筒烟闲谈闲谈罢。怕那倒是更有意思更舒适些。"

华伦已完全不像十五年前法勃里修斯所认识的那个华伦了。可是在法勃里修斯方面却并不因此而减轻他对他的亲爱。他心里满怀了忧虑在守护着他，和一位慈父的守护着他的病的爱子一样。他孜孜不倦地在设法想使他的朋友快乐一点。假使可以使他的客人的呆钝的脸上露出一脸满足的微笑来的话，那他就是很大的牺牲也在所不辞的。华伦也早看出了这一层好意，所以当他要和法勃里修斯别去的时候，他就深深被感动似的捏紧了法勃里修斯的手对他说："老友，你只在希望我的好，那我，我也很知道的……请你相信我，对你这好意我是满心在感谢。我们以后总不会再不通闻问的了，我们以后就互相守着罢。我到家之后将严守着和你的通信。"

华伦动身后的没有几天，法勃里修斯接到了一封从美国寄来的给华伦的信。信封上的略字是"E.H."两字母，——爱伦·霍华德，正是华伦所爱的那女人的名字。法勃里修斯马上将这信转给华伦，并且写上了一句话说："我希望你在这里能接到从美国来的喜音。"——华伦在回信里对这一句话并不提及，并且也完全没有讲到爱伦的事情上去。他只将他现在弄得很舒服的那所他的新住宅的样子说得很清楚，而在邀法勃里修斯就到他那边去见他，可以多住些时。在往后继续的通信当中，两位朋友就约定冬假里耶稣圣诞节和新年，当在一块儿住着过去。

十二月初头上，华伦又写信给法勃里修斯，促他务必要早一点动身。"我身体不好"——在那信里说——"我有时候觉得衰弱到房门也不能出一步。我在此地并没有一个人认识，并且也没有去结识新相知的心思。你和我在一道能使我感到无上的快乐。又和你相习惯了，无论什么地方我都少你不得。我已经为你准备好一间房在这里，你可以自由自在地和在 L……市（莱比锡）一样地工作的，或者也许会比你自己的房子更清静些。你不要等到二十三日才来罢，愈早愈好。我们可以不必等到十二月二十五，就是在十二月十五难道不是一样地可以庆祝耶稣的圣诞的么？"

法勃里修斯也没有什么事情，正在可以适从他朋友的愿望的地位之下，所以就于十二月的初旬里到了他的朋友那里。他觉得他朋友瘦得太厉害，样子太难看了。华伦还没有去看过医生，并且他也拒绝去看病。

"医生能把我怎么样呢？"他说，"我自家的病苦难道会不晓得的么？我并且也很晓得我的病源。医生大约不过会劝我散散心罢了，正譬如他对一个穷苦的病人，劝他吃吃丰美的食物，和陈年的好酒一样。可是穷人哪里有这些必要的钱呢？我们为身体的健康起见，有些物事是不能够一定常办得到的。——譬如我，叫我如何地去散心呢？——去旅行么？——我觉得世上无论什么都没有比这个安逸的静坐更好的事情。——去结识些新的朋友，见见生人的面孔么？——那我觉得世上只有你一个人，只有和你在一道能比一个人的枯坐好些，此外更没有第二个人了。——看书么？——我哪里还有求智识的欲念？我所晓得的东西，对我都已经失掉了兴趣了。"

法勃里修斯，和在与华伦初次遇到的时候一样，注意到了他不吃什么东西而只喜欢喝很多的酒。他对于好友的健康上的忧心，鼓起了他向华伦进劝的勇气。

"你的话原是不错，"华伦回答他说，"我喝酒喝得太多，可是我不能吃旁的东西，而又觉得不得不咽些东西下去以维持我的气力。我是和轧伐尼（Gavarni）的感情残疾者（invalides du sentiment）的可悲的状态一样；'Toutes ces bétises mont dérangéla constitution.'（'原只是那万种的愚行损伤了我的元气'）。"

有一天晚上，窗外面正风狂雨骤，而他们朋友俩却对坐在舒适温暖的房里的时候，华伦忽而讲起了爱伦身上的事情。

"我们现在是不断地在通信了，"他说，"她写信给我说，她希望不久就可以和我再见。——

海耳曼，你晓得么？女人的心理，我实是有点不懂起来了。她不把我当作她的第一个最要好的人看待，那是确实无疑的。——那么为什么她又想和我发生起关系来呢？——为恋爱么？——就是光这一个想头也是可笑得很的。——大约是为了怜悯我的原因罢。——可是这就到了我的矜持的梦的末路了，我已经变了一个怜悯的对象了呵。所以我写信给她说，我已经在此地定住下了，今后别无他望，只想在无为与隐遁中间过我这无用的一生。绝不会和她再见了……你还记得海涅（Heine）的旅行记里的那一段么？一位大学生在窗口和一位美丽的小姑娘亲嘴的那一段？这位小姑娘让他来亲嘴，就因为他说：'明天我又将远去，今生今世怕再也不能和你相见。'——这一个再也不至相见的想头，却使人会得着一种勇气，能说出平时是惹也不敢惹着的事情的。——我觉得我的死期近了。——亲爱的老友，请你不必再说别的话来宽慰我。——我自家是晓得的，死期近了。我也将这事写信给爱伦告诉她了。……我更写了许多另外的事情……嗳，真是些没意思的事情！……我平生所做的，都只是些无用的无目的的事情罢了。到了这垂死的病中，才向情人来宣布恋爱，这岂不是和我的一生很调和很合理的一个结局么？——比这事实更无意识的徒劳，世上还寻得出第二件么？——可是我却如此做了。"

关于这信的事情，法勃里修斯实在想知道得更详细一点，可是华伦却不愿意做断然的回答。——"假如我有一张誊清的信稿在这里的话，"他说，"那我很愿意将它给你去看。你已经知道这事情的全部经过了，我对于自己做出来的那一种愚劣的事情，不管它是如何的无聊如何的笨大，我在你的面前却可以不感到羞缩。——当我在第一次很确实地觉得死期近了的时候，就写了那一封信，这是两礼拜前头的事情。那时候我睡在床上发烧。我对于死是一点儿恐怖也没有的，实际上即使把我的生命交给了死的手里，和现在的这种状态比较起来，也未见得生比死好。可是我却兴奋了，精神亢进了。简直是可以做一部非常之有诗意的作品———篇辞世之歌——出来的样子。我现在还在想这信写了也好。非但如此，我并且还在喜欢，因为爱伦终究知道了我是如何

地爱过她的。既不将我的爱对她陈诉，也不希望
着她对我之爱的给予，——我觉得这是很高尚，
不利己的爱！"

　　圣诞节的祭日一天天地在静默里悲哀里过去
了。华伦变得一天只有几个钟头可以从床上坐起
来那么的衰弱。法勃里修斯现在只能独断地去为
他请了一个医生来到病床前来看他的病。可是诊
察之下，华伦也没有什么一定的病症。是他的生
命力消失完了。他同一盏烧烬的灯火似的在那里
慢慢地萎灭下去。还有几次很少很少的但是间隔
时间却渐渐地比较长起来的间歇时间里，他的精
神又会奋燃起来放几朵火花；但死的阴影已经笼
罩住他，渐渐地渐渐地在暗下去黑下去了。

　　在除夕的当夜，华伦于十一点钟的时候从床
上立了起来。"这一个新年我将照旧式的对你述
祝贺之辞，"他对法勃里修斯说，"希望这新年能
给你以快乐。给我以永久的和平。"

　　将近半夜的时候，他走上钢琴的前头，很庄
严地弹奏起和教会里的合唱歌相像的罗伯特·舒
曼（Robert Schumann）的《死友的饮盏之歌》
（*Auf das Trinkglass eines verstorbenen Freundes*）

来。——寺院里的钟敲十二下的时候，他倒满了
两杯酒。举起杯来，他慢慢地在追思似的，从他
刚才所奏的歌里，谱诵出了一节的歌：

　　　　我在你杯底之所见，

　　　　并非是凡人能解的东西。

　　　　（Was ich ershau'in deinem Grund,

　　　　Yst nicht gewoehnlichen zu nennen.）


　　然后他靠转了背，一长饮就把那满杯干下
了。——他当在说那一节歌和饮那一杯酒的中间，
并不曾对法勃里修斯注意到。法勃里修斯只是悲
哀无语默默地在旁边看着他。现在他看到了法勃
里修斯了，他的眼睛又光明喜乐地充满了少年的
热情。

　　"再喝一杯！"他叫着说："为祝我俩的刎颈
的交情！祝你新年如意，我的哥哥！"

　　他同干头一杯似的将第二杯也干了，然后就
很沉重地在一张椅子上倒了下去。他的目光又变
得呆滞无神了，法勃里修斯扶他到床上去的时
候，他就像一个已经是很想睡的小孩，好好地顺

从了一切。

　　以后几天他一直不能起来。医生来看了也只深思着摇摇头，没有法子好想。他以为法勃里修斯是华伦的近亲，所以告诉法勃里修斯说，还是预备后事罢。

　　正月初八，华伦的别庄所在的那个小市里的旅馆里有一个人差来，来送一封给华伦的信。使者说，这信是要即答的。法勃里修斯因为他朋友已经有好几个钟头陷入了昏睡状态，差不多就快完全失去知觉了，所以就替他开了这信。信的署名者是"爱伦·霍华德"，内容如下：


　　　　父亲在好久之前计划中的欧洲旅行，这一回忽然实现了。我所以不预先通知你以此事者，原想使你惊喜一回，可以开一回玩笑。到了此地，我听逆旅的主人所说，才知道你在前回信里所说的病症还没有离身。因此我所以不愿不通知你而突然前来，并且先要问问你，你的病状究竟能否应许你接待我们？在此地的是我和弗兰息斯，他也和我一样，硬想和你，我的尊敬的朋友，在这一个巡游的途上来相见见，盘桓几天。父亲已经从汉堡直行上巴黎去了，我和弟弟打算在此地住几日后，马上上那里去和他一道的。

　　法勃里修斯想了一想。然后就拿上帽子对使者说，他想自己直接去传达回音。——到了那小旅馆里，他就马上被介绍给了那位外国夫人。他曾先把名片交给一位旅馆的用人，嘱他去说，是受了"华伦博士之托"而来的。

　　爱伦只有一个人在那里。法勃里修斯很快地看了她一遍。她真是美丽得同花一般的样儿。她的一双大大的碧眼很不安地带问似的在注视着这进她房里来的人。

　　法勃里修斯生平和妇人来往得很少，在妇人面前，大抵是局促不安的。可是这时候他的想头已全集中在病友的身上了，所以这一回他倒完全是平静得很的。他只简洁地说了几句话，华伦是病了，——病得很凶——就快死了，给他朋友的信是他拆开了读的。

　　爱伦默默地也有几分惊惶似的朝他看看。她仿佛是不能了解所听见的话的意思的样子。可是慢慢地她的眼睛里就充满起眼泪来了。

"可以许我去见见华伦先生么?"最后她问着说。

法勃里修斯答应了。

"我的弟弟可不可以和我一道去,或者还是我一个人去好些?"

"我觉得还是先由你一个人去好些。你的弟弟或者可以迟一点去看我们那位可怜的朋友的。"

"我突然去看他,一种惊异,不会使病人更衰弱而失神么?"

"大约是不会的。凡一种喜悦,对他总只有好的影响。我晓得他是很喜欢见你的。"

爱伦在几分钟之后就准备好跟法勃里修斯前去,不多一忽,两个人就都到了华伦的屋里了。法勃里修斯教爱伦在客室等了一等,他一个人先到华伦的病房里去。

华伦张大了两只被体热蒸烧得红红的大眼躺在那里。他在那里说昏话了,可是他还能认清这进来者是谁,他向他要求,要一点可以消渴的饮料。他把渴消了以后,就闭上了眼睛,仿佛是要睡了。

"我为你接了一位你的好朋友来，"法勃里修斯说，"你愿意见他么？"

"是不是法勃里修斯？——请他进来罢，欢迎之至！"

"不是的。——是从美国来的朋友。"

"从美国？……在那里我是住得很久，很久，……啊，那沉郁的，悲哀的两岸！……"

"你愿不愿意见你那朋友？"

"我航下了那条暗淡的河流——航下了。在雾蒙蒙的远处呢：高高的、黑暗的形状；茂树的高山；……我是再也……再也达不到的远处。"

法勃里修斯踮起了脚尖，轻轻离开了他，几分钟后又和爱伦一道走进这病房来了。华伦似乎仍旧是什么也不晓得的样子。他只是用了轻轻的，声气也没有的喉音在说：

"这暗淡的河流，渐渐地到海了。我听见有海里的钝重的浪声。两岸是绿色的。高山也移近前来了。那是树林，我曾在它们之下常常息躺着的树林……树林的黑暗……在这些树木之间却浮出来了一个辉耀的女身……爱伦！"

她踏近了他的床边。这将死者一点儿也没有

惊异，只和蔼地朝她看。

"天呀天！我还能见到你！"他说，"我晓得你是会来的。"他又喃喃说了些听不清的话；然后静躺了好久。忽而他又叫起来说："海耳曼！"

被叫者就站在爱伦的边上。

"那个幸福的摆！你明白么？"——一种无邪的同小孩子似的笑容飞过他的脸上，他将瘦得只剩了皮骨的一只右手举得高高，用食指在空中画了半个摆动的大圈，又追加着说："从前是这样的！"然后又同样地自右到左，慢慢地画了几次短小的半圈，说："现在！"——最后同威胁人似的又将手指停住，坚决而不动地在空中指着："即刻！"——于是他闭上了眼睛，很苦地呼吸了几口气，默默地静躺着了。

爱伦一边哭着，一边将身体俯伏了下去轻轻地叫说："亨利！亨利！"他又将衰弱极了的眼睛开了一次。她将嘴凑近了他的耳边，如泉地涌流着眼泪，轻轻地向他耳里说："我是爱你的，老早就爱你的，还没有把你忘记过。"

"我也老早就晓得了，"华伦很平静地很有自信似的回答说。——他脸上的呆滞的表情立刻就变得和润了一点，有了一点生气。眼睛也很亲爱似的，密呢似的发起光来了，和许多年前的时候一样。他拿住了爱伦的手，将它拿上了已经是枯燥了的唇边。一脸微笑流露在他的脸上。

"现在你觉得怎么样？"法勃里修斯问他。

"很好很好……"又是那个旧日的回答。他的无力的手指向被单上摸捏了一回，仿佛是想将这被单扯拖举起来的样子。然后将手臂长长地伸上放落，手指也静止地摊着不动了。——"很好很好……"他还轻轻地说了一遍。他似乎沉没在深远的回忆里。一个长时间的沉默闯入在三人之间。最后又充满了热意和悲哀将他的已经在散神的眼睛举起，对他的爱人看着，极轻极轻地，嗫嚅地，将一个无力的重音摆在头一个字上，说了一声："很——好。"

★　★　★　★　★

上面所译的，是德国Rudolf Lindau所著的小说 *Das Glueckspendel*。

小说里的许多原名，把它们写在下面：

主人公是 Heinrich Warren。他的朋友是 Hermann Fabricius。女主人公是 Ellen Gilmore。她的兄弟是 Francis Gilmore。她的男人是 Mr. Howard。

华伦出生的地方是德国的 Talbe an der Saale。教书的地方是纽约州的 Mira。从 Liverpool 到纽约的船名是 Atlantic。

德国有一种货币名 Taler，——"泰来"大约有中国的一块五角钱那么的价值。

译者所根据的书，是柏林 Buchverlag fuers Deutsche Haus 在一九〇九年出版的 *Die Buecher des Deutschen Hauses* 丛书的第五辑第一百零三种。据这丛书的第四辑第九十八本的 *Erzaehlungen aus dem Osten*（von Rudolf Lindau）绪言里之所说，则林道系于一八二九年十月十日生在 Gardelegen in der Altmark。大了就在柏林，巴黎，及 Montpellier 等处修习言语学与史学。到他的学业修完之后，他还在法国南部住了四年，做人家的家庭教师。然后就做了法国公使 Barthéléme St. Hillaire 的秘书。一八六〇年瑞士国把他当作了外交官派赴日本，去结两国间的通商条约。因此他得到了一个总领事的资格，到一八六九年为止，就来往分驻在印度，新加坡，中国，日本，及加利福尼亚等处。在法国的时候，他已经开始他的文士生活在*Revue des deux Mondes*及*Journal des Dè bates*杂志上投稿了。他的第一篇旅行记*Voyage autour du Japon*就是用法文写的。后来在横滨，他发行了最初的英字新闻纸，有一卷英文短篇小说，却是用英文写的。

一八七〇年以后到一八七二年为止，他往还于德国及东方，做战地的记者。一八七二年到一八七八年之间，他住在巴黎，做德国使馆的馆员。一八八〇到一八八五年他做了使馆的参赞。一八九二年德国派干员出外，他就又做了一次德国的代表赴君士坦丁之任。归休之后，他就在Helgoland住下了。一八九三年，他出了六卷的全集。他死在巴黎，一九一〇年的十月十四葬在Helgoland。

在短篇小说方面，他先在一八六九年（当他在三十九岁的时候）出了一本法文短篇小说集，名*Peines perdues*，系从前在*Revue des deux Mondes*与*Journal de St Petersberg*杂志上所发表的东西。他用英文写的，在*Blackwood's Magazine*上所发表的东西。又收集了起来，都归入在*The Philosopher's Pendulum and other Stories*这一个书名之下。德国的全集的书名很多，这儿不能一一举出，但*The Philosoper's Pendulum*一篇，则当然是由他自己译成德文的无疑。所以我想英文的原作与德文的原作，少许有点出入也是应该的。

一九二八年六月

# The Philosopher's Pendulum[1]

## by Rudolf Lindau

## I

During many long years Hermann Fabricius had lost sight of his friend Henry Warren, and had forgotten him.

Yet when students together they had loved each other dearly, and more than once they had sworn eternal friendship. This was at a period which, though not very remote, we seem to have left far behind us—a time when young men still believed in eternal friendship, and could feel enthusiasm for great deeds

---

①《幸福的摆》中文译文由郁达夫根据所甄选的德语版本翻译而成。这篇为读者提供的英文对照原文,是由R.林道本人根据自己德语版翻成的英文版,与德文版相比照,个别细节有出入。

or great ideas. Youth in the present day is, or thinks itself, more rational. Hermann and Warren in those days were simple-minded and ingenuous; and not only in the moment of elation, when they had sworn to be friends for ever, but even the next day, and the day after that, in sober earnestness, they had vowed that nothing should separate them, and that they would remain united through life. The delusion had not lasted long. The pitiless machinery of life had caught up the young men as soon as they left the university, and had thrown one to the right, the other to the left. For a few months they had exchanged long and frequent letters; then they had met once, and finally they had parted, each going his way. Their letters had become more scarce, more brief, and at last had ceased altogether. It would really seem that the fact of having interests in common is the one thing sufficiently powerful to prolong and keep up the life of epistolary relations. A man may feel great affection for an absent friend, and yet not find time to write him ten lines, while he will willingly expend daily many hours on a stranger from whom he expects something. None the less he may be a true and honest friend. Man is naturally selfish; the instinct of self-preservation requires it of him. Provided he be not wicked, and that he show himself ready to serve his neighbor—after himself—no one has a right to complain, or to accuse him of hard-heartedness.

At the time this story begins, Hermann had even forgotten whether he had written to Warren last, or whether he had left his friend's last letter unanswered. In a word, the correspondence which began so enthusiastically had entirely ceased. Hermann inhabited a large town, and had acquired some reputation as a writer. From time to time, in the course of his walks, he would meet a young student with brown hair, and mild, honest-looking blue eyes, whose countenance, with its frank and youthful smile, inspired confidence and invited the sympathy of the passer-by. Whenever Hermann met this young man he would say to himself, "How like Henry at twenty!" and for a few minutes memory would travel back to the already distant days of youth, and he would long to see his dear old Warren again. More than once, on the spur of the moment, he had resolved to try and find out what had become of his old university comrade. But these good intentions were never followed up. On reaching home he would find his table covered with books and pamphlets to be reviewed, and letters from publishers or newspaper editors asking for "copy"—to say nothing of invitations to dinner, which must be accepted or refused; in a word, he found so much URGENT business to despatch that the evening would go by, and weariness would overtake him, before he could make time for inquiring about his old friend.

In the course of years, the life of most men becomes so regulated that no time is left for anything beyond "necessary work". But, indeed, the man who lives only for his own pleasure—doing, so to speak, nothing—is rarely better in this respect than the writer, the banker, and the savant, who are overburdened with work.

One afternoon, as Hermann, according to his custom, was returning home about five o'clock, his porter handed him a letter bearing the American post-mark. He examined it closely before opening it. The large and rather stiff handwriting on the address seemed familiar, and yet he could not say to whom it belonged. Suddenly his countenance brightened, and he exclaimed, "A letter from Henry!" He tore open the envelope, and read as follows:

"MY DEAR HERMANN,—It is fortunate that one of us at least should have attained celebrity. I saw your name on the outside of a book of which you are the author. I wrote at once to the publisher; that obliging man answered me by return of post, and, thanks to these circumstances, I am enabled to tell you that I will land at Hamburg towards the end of September. Write to me there, Poste Restante, and let me know if you are willing to receive me for a few days. I can take Leipzig on my way home, and would do so most willingly if you say that you would see me again with pleasure.

Your old friend,

HENRY WARREN."

Below the signature there was a postscript of a single line: "This is my present face." And from an inner envelope Hermann drew a small photograph, which he carried to the window to examine leisurely. As he looked, a painful impression of sadness came over him. The portrait was that of an old man. Long gray hair fell in disorder over a careworn brow; the eyes, deep sunk in their sockets, had a strange and disquieting look of fixity; and the mouth, surrounded by deep furrows, seemed to tell its own long tale of sorrow.

"Poor Henry!" said Hermann, "this, then, is your present face! And yet he is not old; he is younger than I am; he can scarcely be thirty-eight. Can I, too, be already an old man?"

He walked up to the glass, and looked attentively at the reflection of his own face. No! Those were not the features of a man whose life was near its close;

the eye was bright, and the complexion indicated vigor and health. Still, it was not a young face. Thought and care had traced their furrows round the mouth and about the temples, and the general expression was one of melancholy, not to say despondency.

"Well, well, we have grown old," said Hermann, with a sigh. "I had not thought about it this long while; and now this photograph has reminded me of it painfully." Then he took up his pen and wrote to say how happy he would be to see his old friend again as soon as possible.

The next day chance brought him face to face in the street with the young student who was so like Warren. "Who knows?" thought Hermann, "fifteen or twenty years hence this young man may look no brighter than Warren does today. Ah, life is not easy! It has a way of saddening joyous looks, and imparting severity to smiling lips. As for me, I have no real right to complain of my life. I have lived pretty much like everybody; a little satisfaction, and then a little disappointment, turn by turn; and often small worries; and so my youth has gone by, I scarcely know how."

On the 2nd of October Hermann received a telegram from Hamburg announcing the arrival of Warren for the same evening. At the appointed hour he went to the railway station to meet his friend. He saw him get down from the carriage slowly, and rather heavily, and he watched him for a few seconds before accosting him. Warren appeared to him old and broken-down, and even more feeble than he had expected to see him from his portrait. He wore a travelling suit of gray cloth, so loose and wide that it hung in folds on the gaunt and stooping figure; a large wide-awake hat was drawn down to his very eyes. The new-comer looked right and left, seeking no doubt to discover his friend; not seeing him, he turned his weary and languid steps towards the way out. Hermann then came forward. Warren recognized him at once; a sunny, youthful smile lighted up his countenance, and, evidently much moved, he stretched out his hand. An hour later, the two friends were seated opposite to each other before a well-spread table in Hermann's comfortable apartments.

Warren ate very little; but, on the other hand, Hermann noticed with surprise and some anxiety that his friend, who had been formerly a model of sobriety, drank a good deal. Wine, however, seemed to have no effect on him. The pale face did not flush; there was the same cold, fixed look in the eye; and his speech, though slow and dull in tone, betrayed no embarrassment.

When the servant who had waited at dinner had taken away the dessert and brought in coffee, Hermann wheeled two big arm-chairs close to the fire, and said to his friend. "Now, we will not be interrupted. Light a cigar, make yourself at home, and tell me all you have been doing since we parted."

Warren pushed away the cigars. "If you do not mind," said he, "I will smoke my pipe. I am used to it, and I prefer it to the best of cigars."

So saying, he drew from its well-worn case an old

pipe, whose color showed it had been long used, and filled it methodically with moist, blackish tobacco. Then he lighted it, and after sending forth one or two loud puffs of smoke, he said, with an air of sovereign satisfaction.

"A quiet, comfortable room—a friend—a good pipe after dinner—and no care for the morrow. That's what I like."

Hermann cast a sidelong glance at his companion, and was painfully struck at his appearance. The tall gaunt frame in its stooping attitude; the grayish hair and sad, fixed look; the thin legs crossed one over the other; the elbow resting on the knee and supporting the chin,—in a word, the whole strange figure, as it sat there, bore no resemblance to Henry Warren, the friend of his youth. This man was a stranger, a mysterious being even. Nevertheless, the affection he felt for his friend was not impaired; on the contrary, pity entered into his heart. "How ill the world must have used him," thought Hermann, "to have thus disfigured him!" Then he said aloud, "Now, then, let me have your story, unless you prefer to hear mine first."

He strove to speak lightly, but he felt that the effort was not successful. As to Warren, he went on smoking quietly, without saying a word. The long silence at last became painful. Hermann began to feel an uncomfortable sensation of distress in presence of the strange guest he had brought to his home. After a few minutes he ventured to ask for the third time, "Will you make up your mind to speak, or must I begin?"

Warren gave vent to a little noiseless laugh. "I am thinking how I can answer your question. The difficulty is that, to speak truly, I have absolutely nothing to tell. I wonder now—and it was that made me pause—how it has happened that, throughout my life, I have been bored by—nothing. As if it would not have been quite as natural, quite as easy, and far pleasanter, to have been amused by that same nothing—which has been my life. The fact is, my dear fellow, that I have had no deep sorrow to bear, neither have I been happy. I have not been extraordinarily successful, and have drawn none of the prizes of life. But I am well aware that, in this respect, my lot resembles that of thousands of other men. I have always been obliged to work. I have earned my bread by the sweat of my brow. I have had money difficulties; I have even had a hopeless passion—but what then? Every one has had that. Besides, that was in bygone days; I have learned to bear it, and to forget. What pains and angers me is, to have to confess that my life has been spent without satisfaction and without happiness."

He paused an instant, and then resumed, more calmly. "A few years ago I was foolish enough to believe that things might in the end turn out better. I was a professor with a very moderate salary at the school at Elmira. I taught all I knew, and much that I had to learn in order to be able to teach it—Greek and Latin, German and French, mathematics and physical sciences. During the so-called play-hours, I even gave music lessons. In the course of the whole day there were few moments of liberty for me. I was perpetually surrounded by a crowd of rough, ill-bred boys, whose only object during lessons was to catch me making a fault in English. When evening came, I was quite worn out; still, I could always find time to dream for half an hour or so with my eyes open before going to bed. Then all my desires were accomplished, and I was supremely happy. At last I had drawn a prize! I was successful in everything; I was rich, honored, powerful—what more can I say? I astonished the world—or rather, I astonished Ellen Gilmore, who for me was the whole world. Hermann, have you ever been as mad? Have you, too, in a waking dream, been in turn a statesman, a millionaire, the author of a sublime work, a victorious general, the head of a great political party? Have you dreamt nonsense such as that? I, who am here, have been all I say—in dreamland. Never mind; that was a good time. Ellen Gilmore, whom I have just mentioned, was the eldest sister of one of my pupils, Francis Gilmore, the most undisciplined boy of the school. His parents, nevertheless, insisted on his learning something; and as I had the reputation of possessing unwearying patience, I was selected to give him private lessons. That was how I obtained a footing in the Gilmore family. Later on, when they had found out that I was somewhat of a musician—you may remember, perhaps, that for an amateur I was a tolerable performer on the piano—I went every day to the house to teach Latin and Greek to Francis, and music to Ellen.

"Now, picture to yourself the situation, and then laugh at your friend as he has laughed at himself many a time. On the one side—the Gilmore side— a large fortune and no lack of pride; an intelligent, shrewd, and practical father; an ambitious and vain mother; an affectionate but spoilt boy; and a girl of nineteen, surpassingly lovely, with a cultivated mind and great good sense. On the other hand, you have Henry Warren, aged twenty-nine; in his dreams the author of a famous work, or the commander-in-chief of the Northern armies, or, it may be, President of the

Republic—in reality, Professor at Elmira College, with a modest stipend of seventy dollars a month. Was it not evident that the absurdity of my position as a suitor for Ellen would strike me at once? Of course it did. In my lucid moments, when I was not dreaming, I was a very rational man, who had read a good deal, and learned not a little; and it would have been sheer madness in me to have indulged for an instant the hope of a marriage between Ellen and myself. I knew it was an utter impossibility—as impossible as to be elected President of the United States; and yet, in spite of myself, I dreamed of it. However, I must do myself the justice to add that my passion inconvenienced nobody. I would no more have spoken of it than of my imaginary command of the army of the Potomac. The pleasures which my love afforded me could give umbrage to no one. Yet I am convinced that Ellen read my secret. Not that she ever said a word to me on the subject; no look or syllable of hers could have made me suspect that she had guessed the state of my mind.

"One single incident I remember which was not in accordance with her habitual reserve in this respect. I noticed one day that her eyes were red. Of course I dared not ask her why she had cried. During the lesson she seemed absent; and when leaving she said, without looking at me, 'I may perhaps be obliged to interrupt our lessons for some little time; I am very sorry. I wish you every happiness.' Then, without raising her eyes, she quickly left the room. I was bewildered. What could her words mean? And why had they been said in such an affectionate tone?

"The next day Francis Gilmore called to inform me, with his father's compliments, that he was to have four days' holidays, because his sister had just been betrothed to Mr. Howard, a wealthy New York merchant, and that, for the occasion, there would be great festivities at home.

"Thenceforward there was an end of the dreams which up to that moment had made life pleasant. In sober reason I had no more cause to deplore Ellen's marriage than to feel aggrieved because Grant had succeeded Johnson as President. Nevertheless, you can scarcely conceive how much this affair—I mean the marriage—grieved me. My absolute nothingness suddenly stared me in the face. I saw myself as I was—a mere schoolmaster, with no motive for pride in the past, or pleasure in the present, or hope in the future."

Warren's pipe had gone out while he was telling his story. He cleaned it out methodically, drew from his pocket a cake of Cavendish tobacco, and, after cutting off with a penknife the necessary quantity, refilled his pipe and lit it. The way in which he performed all these little operations betrayed long habit. He had ceased to speak while he was relighting his pipe, and kept on whistling between his teeth. Hermann looked on—silently. After a few minutes, and when the pipe was in good order, Warren resumed his story.

"For a few weeks I was terribly miserable; not so much because I had lost Ellen—a man cannot lose what he has never hoped to possess—as from the ruin of all my illusions. During those days I plucked and ate by the dozen of the fruits of the tree of self-knowledge, and I found them very bitter. I ended by leaving Elmira, to seek my fortunes elsewhere. I knew my trade well. Long practice had taught me how to make the best of my learning, and I never had any difficulty in finding employment. I taught successively in upwards of a dozen States of the Union. I can scarcely recollect the names of all the places where I have lived—Sacramento, Chicago, St. Louis, Cincinnati, Boston, New York; I have been everywhere—everywhere. And everywhere I have met with the same rude schoolboys, just as I have found the same regular and irregular verbs in Latin and Greek. If you would see a man thoroughly satiated and saturated with schoolboys and classical grammars, look at me.

"In the leisure time which, whatever might be my work, I still contrived to make for myself, I indulged in philosophical reflections. Then it was I took to the habit of smoking so much."

Warren stopped suddenly, and, looking straight before him, appeared plunged in thought. Then, passing his hand over his forehead, he repeated, in an absent manner, "Yes, of smoking so much. I also took to another habit," he added, somewhat hastily; "but that has nothing to do with my story. The theory which especially occupied my thoughts was that of the oscillations of an ideal instrument of my own imagining, to which, in my own mind, I gave the name of the Philosopher's Pendulum. To this invention I owe the quietude of mind which has supported me for many years, and which, as you see, I now enjoy. I said to myself that my great sorrow—if I may so call it without presumption—had arisen merely from my wish to be extraordinarily happy. When, in his dreams, a man has carried presumption so far as to attain to the heights of celebrity, or to being the husband of Ellen Gilmore, there was nothing wonderful if, on awaking, he sustained a heavy fall before reaching the depths of reality. Had I been less ambitious in my desires, their realization would have been easier, or, at any rate, the disappointment would have been less bitter. Starting from this principle, I arrived at the logical conclusion that the best means to avoid being unhappy is to wish for as little happiness as possible. This truth was discovered by my philosophical forefathers many centuries before the birth of Christ, and I lay no claim to being the finder of it; but the outward symbol which I ended by giving to this idea is—at least I fancy it is—of my invention.

"Give me a sheet of paper and a pencil," he added, turning to his friend, "and with a few lines I can demonstrate clearly the whole thing."

Hermann handed him what he wanted without a word. Warren then began gravely to draw a large semicircle, open at the top, and above the semicircular line a pendulum, which fell perpendicularly and touched the circumference at the exact point where on the dial of a clock would be inscribed the figure VI. This done, he wrote on the right-hand side of the pendulum, beginning from the bottom and at the places of the hours V, IV, III, the words Moderate Desires—Great Hopes, Ambition—Unbridled Passion, Mania of Greatness. Then, turning the paper upside-down, he wrote on the opposite side, where on a dial would be marked VII, VIII, IX, the words Slight Troubles—Deep Sorrow, Disappointment— Despair. Lastly, in the place of No. VI, just where the pendulum fell, he sketched a large black spot, which he shaded off with great care, and above which he wrote, like a scroll, Dead Stop, Absolute Repose.

Having finished this little drawing, Warren laid down his pipe, inclined his head on one side, and raising his eyebrows, examined his work with a critical frown. "This compass is not yet quite complete," he said; "there is something missing. Between Dead Stop and Moderate Desires on the right, and Slight Troubles on the left, there is the beautiful line of Calm and Rational Indifference. However, such as the drawing is, it is sufficient to demonstrate my theory. Do you follow me?"

Hermann nodded affirmatively. He was greatly

pained. In lieu of the friend of his youth, for whom he had hoped a brilliant future, here was a poor monomaniac!

"You see," said Warren, speaking collectedly, like a professor, "if I raise my pendulum till it reaches the point of Moderate Desires and then let it go, it will naturally swing to the point of Slight Troubles, and go no further. Then it will oscillate for some time in a more and more limited space on the line of Indifference, and finally it will stand still without any jerk on Dead Stop, Absolute Repose. That is a great consolation!"

He paused, as if waiting for some remark from Hermann; but as the latter remained silent, Warren resumed his demonstration.

"You understand now, I suppose, what I am coming to. If I raise the pendulum to the point of Ambition or Mania of Greatness, and then let it go, that same law which I have already applied will drive it to Deep Sorrow or Despair. That is quite clear, is it not?"

"Quite clear," repeated Hermann sadly.

"Very well," continued Warren, with perfect gravity, "for my misfortune, I discovered this fine theory rather late. I had not set bounds to my dreams and limited them to trifles. I had wished to be President of the Republic, an illustrious savant, the husband of Ellen. No great things, eh? What say you to my modesty? I had raised the pendulum to such a giddy height that when it slipped from my impotent hands it naturally performed a long oscillation, and touched the point Despair. That was a miserable time. I hope you have never suffered what I suffered then. I lived in a perpetual nightmare—like the stupor at intoxication." He paused, as he had done before, and then, with a painfully nervous laugh, he added, "Yes, like intoxication. I drank." Suddenly a spasm seemed to pass over his face, he looked serious and sad as before, and he said, with a shudder, "It's a terrible thing to see one's self inwardly, and to know that one is fallen."

After this he remained long silent. At last, raising

his head, he turned to his friend and said, "Have you had enough of my story, or would you like to hear it to the end?"

"I am grieved at all you have told me," said Hermann, "but pray go on; it is better I should know all."

"Yes, and I feel, too, that it relieves me to pour out my heart. Well, I used to drink. One takes to the horrid habit in America far easier than anywhere else. I was obliged to give up more than one good situation because I had ceased to be RESPECTABLE. Anyhow, I always managed to find employment without any great difficulty. I never suffered from want, though I have never known plenty. If I spent too much in drink, I took it out of my dress and my boots.

"Eighteen months after I had left Elmira, I met Ellen one day in Central Park, in New York. I was aware that she had been married a twelve-month. She knew me again at once, and spoke to me. I would have wished to sink into the earth. I knew that my clothes were shabby, that I looked poor, and I fancied that she must discern on my face the traces of the bad habits I had contracted. But she did not, or would not, see anything. She held out her hand, and said in her gentle voice.

'I am very glad to see you again, Mr. Warren. I have inquired about you, but neither my father nor Francis could tell me what had become of you. I want to ask you to resume the lessons you used to give me. Perhaps you do not know where I live? This is my address,' and she gave me her card.

"I stammered out a few unmeaning words in reply to her invitation. She looked at me, smiling kindly the while; but suddenly the smile vanished, and she added, 'Have you been ill, Mr. Warren? You seem worn.'

"'Yes,' I answered, too glad to find an excuse for my appearance—'yes, I have been ill, and I am still suffering.'

"'I am very sorry,' she said, in a low voice.

"Laugh at me, Hermann—call me an incorrigible

madman; but believe me when I say that her looks conveyed to me the impression of more than common interest or civility. A thrilling sense of pain shot through my frame. What had I done that I should be so cruelly tried? A mist passed before my eyes; anxiety, intemperance, sleeplessness, had made me weak. I tottered backwards a few steps. She turned horribly pale. All around us was the crowd—the careless, indifferent crowd.

"'Come and see me soon,' she added hastily, and left me. I saw her get into a carriage, which she had doubtless quitted to take a walk; and when she drove past, she put her head out and looked at me with her eyes wide open—there was an almost wildly anxious expression in them.

"I went home. My way led me past her house—it was a palace. I shut myself up in my wretched hotel-room, and once more I fell to dreaming. Ellen loved me; she admired me; she was not for ever lost to me! The pendulum was swinging, you see, up as high as Madness. Explain to me, if you can, how it happens that a being perfectly rational in ordinary life should at certain seasons, and, so to speak, voluntarily, be bereft of reason. To excuse and explain my temporary insanity, I am ready to admit that the excitement to which I gave way may have been a symptom of the nervous malady which laid hold of me a few days later, and stretched me for weeks upon a bed of pain.

"As I became convalescent, reason and composure returned. But it was too late. In the space of two months, twenty years had passed over my head. When I rose from my sick-bed I was as feeble and as broken-down as you see me now. My past had been cheerless and dim, without one ray of happiness; yet that past was all my life! Henceforward there was nothing left for me to undertake, to regret, or to desire. The pendulum swung idly backwards and forwards on the line of Indifference. I wonder what are the feelings of successful men—of men who HAVE been victorious generals, prime ministers, celebrated authors, and that sort of thing! Upheld by a legitimate pride, do they retire satisfied from the lists when evening comes, or do they lay down their arms as I did, disappointed and dejected, and worn out with the fierce struggle? Can no man with impunity look into his own heart and ask himself how his life has been spent?"

Here Warren made a still longer pause than before, and appeared absorbed in gloomy thought. At last he resumed in a lower tone.

"I had not followed up Ellen's invitation. But in some way she had discovered my address, and knew of my illness. Do not be alarmed, my dear Hermann; my story will not become romantic. No heavenly vision appeared to me during my fever; I felt no gentle white hands laid on my burning brow. I was nursed at the hospital, and very well nursed too; I figured there as 'Number 380', and the whole affair was, as you see, as prosaic as possible. But on quitting the hospital, and as I was taking leave of the manager, he handed me a letter, in which was enclosed a note for five hundred dollars. In the envelope there was also the following anonymous note:

"'An old friend begs your acceptance, as a loan, of the inclosed sum. It will be time enough to think of paying off this debt when you are strong enough to resume work, and you can then do it by instalments, of which you can yourself fix the amount, and remit them to the hospital of New York.'

"It was well meant, no doubt, but it caused me a painful impression. My determination was taken at once. I refused without hesitation. I asked the manager, who had been watching me with a friendly smile while I read the letter, whether he could give the name of the person who had sent it. In spite of his repeated assurances that he did not know it, I never doubted for a single instant that he was concealing the truth. After a few seconds' reflection I asked if he would undertake to forward an answer to my unknown correspondent; and, on his consenting to do so, I promised that he should have my answer the next day.

"I thought long over my letter. One thing was plain to me—it was Ellen who had come to my help. How could I reject her generous aid without wounding her or appearing ungrateful? After great hesitation I wrote a few lines, which, as far as I can recollect, ran thus:

"'I thank you for the interest you have shown me, but it is impossible for me to accept the sum you place at my disposal. Do not be angry with me because I return it. Do not withdraw your sympathy; I will strive to remain worthy of it, and will never forget your goodness.'

"A few days later, after having confided this letter to the manager, I left New York for San Francisco. For several years I heard nothing of Ellen; her image grew gradually fainter, and at last almost disappeared from my memory.

"The dark river that bore the frail bark which carried me and my fortunes was carrying me smoothly and unconsciously along towards the mysterious abyss where all that exists is engulfed.

Its course lay through a vast desert; and the banks which passed before my eyes were of fearful sameness. Indescribable lassitude took possession of my whole being. I had never, knowingly, practised evil; I had loved and sought after good. Why, then, was I so wretched? I would have blessed the rock which wrecked my back so that I might have been swallowed up and have gone down to my eternal rest. Up to the day when I heard of Ellen's betrothal, I had hoped that the morrow would bring happiness. The long-wished-for morrow had come at last, gloomy and colorless, without realizing any of my vague hopes. Henceforth my life was at an end."

Warren said these last words so indistinctly that Hermann could scarcely hear them; he seemed to be speaking to himself rather than to his friend. Then he raised the forefinger of his right hand, and after moving it slowly from right to left, in imitation of the swing of a pendulum, he placed it on the large black dot he had drawn on the sheet of paper exactly below his pendulum, and said, "Dead Stop, Absolute

Repose. Would that the end were come!"

Another and still longer interval of silence succeeded, and at last Hermann felt constrained to speak.

"How came you to make up your mind," he said, "to return to Europe?"

"Ah, yes, to be sure," answered Warren, hurriedly, "the story—the foolish story—is not ended. In truth it has no end, as it had no beginning; it is a thing without form or purpose, and less the history of a life than of a mere journeying towards death. Still I will finish—following chronological order. It does not weary you?"

"No, no; go on, my dear friend."

"Very well. I spent several years in the United States. The pendulum worked well. It came and went, to and fro, slowly along the line of Indifference, without ever transgressing as its extreme limits on either hand, Moderate Desires and Slight Troubles. I led obscurely a contemplative life, and I was generally considered a queer character. I fulfilled my duties, and took little heed of any one. Whenever I had an hour at my disposal, I sought solitude in the neighboring woods, far from the town and from mankind. I used to lie down under the big trees. Every season in turn, spring and summer, autumn and winter, had its peculiar charm for me. My heart, so full of bitterness, felt lightened as soon as I listened to the rustling of the foliage overhead. The forest! There is nothing finer in all creation. A deep calm seemed to settle down upon me. I was growing old. I was forgetting. It was about this time that, in consequence of my complete indifference to all surroundings, I acquired the habit of answering 'Very well' to everything that was said. The words came so naturally that I was not aware of my continual use of them, until one day one of my fellow-teachers happened to tell me that masters and pupils alike had given me the nickname of 'Very well'. Is it not odd that one who has never succeeded in anything should be known as 'Very well'?

"I have only one other little adventure to relate,

and I will have told all. Then I can listen to your story.

"Last year, my journeyings brought me to the neighborhood of Elmira. It was holiday-time. I had nothing to do, and I had in my purse a hundred hardly earned dollars, or thereabout. The wish seized me to revisit the scene of my joys and my sorrows. I had not set foot in the place for more than seven years. I was so changed that nobody could know me again; nor would I have cared much if they had. After visiting the town and looking at my old school, and the house where Ellen had lived, I bent my steps towards the park, which is situated in the environs—a place where I used often to walk in company of my youthful dreams. It was September, and evening was closing in. The oblique rays of the setting sun sent a reddish gleam the leafy branches of the old oaks. I seated on a bench beneath a tree on one side of the path. As I drew near I recognized Ellen. I remained rooted to the spot where I stood, not daring to move a step. She was stooping forward with her head bent down, while with the end of her parasol she traced lines upon the gravel. She had not seen me. I turned back instantly, and retired without making any noise. When I had gone a little distance, I left the path and struck into the wood. Once there, I looked back cautiously. Ellen was still at the same place and in the same attitude. Heaven knows what thoughts passed through my brain! I longed to see her closer. What danger was there? I was sure she would not know me again. I walked towards her with the careless step of a casual passer-by, and in a few minutes passed before her. When my shadow fell on the path, she looked up, and our eyes met. My heart was beating fast. Her look was cold and indifferent; but suddenly a strange light shot into her eyes, and she made a quick movement, as if to rise. I saw no more, and went on without turning round. Before I could get out of the park her carriage drove past me, and I saw her once more as I had seen her five years before in Central Park, pale, with distended eyes, and her anxious looks fixed upon me. Why did I not bow to her? I cannot say; my courage failed me. I saw the light die out of her eyes. I almost fancied that I saw her heave a sigh of relief as she threw herself back carelessly in the carriage; and she disappeared. I was then thirty-six, and I am almost ashamed to relate the schoolboy's trick of which I was guilty. I sent her the following lines: 'A devoted friend, whom you obliged in former days, and who met you yesterday in the park without your recognizing him, sends you his remembrances.' I posted this letter a few minutes before getting into the train which was to take me to New York; and, as I did so, my heart beat as violently as though I had performed a heroic deed. Great adventures, forsooth! And to think that my life presents none more striking, and that trifles such as these are the only food for my memory!

"A twelve-month later I met Francis Gilmore in Broadway. The world is small—so small that it is really difficult to keep out of the way of people one has once known. The likeness of my former pupil to his sister struck me, and I spoke to him. He looked at me at first with a puzzled expression, but after a few moments of hesitation he recognized me, a bright smile lighted up his pleasant face, and he shook hands warmly.

"'Mr. Warren,' he exclaimed, 'how glad I am to see you! Ellen and I have often talked of you, and wondered what could have become of you. Why did we never hear from you?'

"'I did not suppose it would interest you.' I spoke timidly; and yet I owed nothing to the young fellow, and wanted nothing of him.

"'You wrong us by saying that,' replied Francis, 'do you think me ungrateful? Do you fancy I have forgotten our pleasant walks in former days, and the long conversations we used to have? You alone ever taught me anything, and it is to you I owe the principles that have guided me through life. Many a day I have thought of you, and regretted you sincerely. As regards Ellen, no one has ever filled your place with her; she plays to this day the same pieces of music you taught her, and follows all your directions with a fidelity that would touch you.'

'How are your father and mother, and how is your sister?' I inquired, feeling more deeply moved than I can express.

'My poor mother died three years ago. It is Ellen who keeps house now.'

'Your brother-in-law lives with you, then?'

'My brother-in-law!' replied Francis, with surprise, 'did you not know that he was on board the Atlantic, which was lost last year in the passage from Liverpool to New York?'

I could find no words to reply.

'As to that,' added Francis, with great composure—'between you and me, he was no great loss. My dear brother-in-law was not by any means what my father fancied he was when he gave him my sister as a wife. The whole family has often regretted the marriage. Ellen lived apart from her husband for many years before his death.'

I nodded so as to express my interest in his communications, but I could not for words have uttered a syllable.

'You will come and see us soon, I hope,' added Francis, without noticing my emotion. 'We are still at the same place; but to make sure, here is my card. Come, Mr. Warren—name your own day to come and dine with us. I promise you a hearty welcome.'

I got off by promising to write the next day, and we parted."

"Fortunately my mind had lost its former liveliness. The pendulum, far from being urged to unruly motion, continued to swing slowly in the narrow space where it had oscillated for so many years. I said to myself that to renew my intimacy with the Gilmores would be to run the almost certain risk of reviving the sorrows and the disappointments of the past. I was then calm and rational. It would be madness in me, I felt, to aspire to the hand of a young, wealthy, and much admired widow. To venture to see Ellen again was to incur the risk of seeing my reason once more wrecked, and the fatal chimera which had been the source of all my misery start into life again. If we are to believe what poets say, love ennobles man and exalts him into a demigod. It may be so, but it turns him likewise into a fool and a madman. That was my case. At any cost I was to guard against that fatal passion. I argued seriously with myself, and I determined to let the past be, and to reject every opportunity of bringing it to life again."

"A few days before my meeting with Francis, I had received tidings of the death of an old relative, whom I scarcely knew. In my childhood I had, on one or two occasions, spent my holidays at his house. He was gloomy and taciturn, but nevertheless he had always welcomed me kindly. I have a vague remembrance of having been told that he had been in love with my mother once upon a time, and that on hearing of her marriage he had retired into the solitude which he never left till the day of his death. Be that as it may, I had not lost my place in his affections, it seems he had continued to feel an interest in me; and on his deathbed he had remembered me, and left me the greater part of his not very considerable fortune. I inherited little money; but there was a small, comfortably-furnished country-house, and an adjoining farm let on a long lease for two hundred and forty pounds per annum. This was wealth for me, and more than enough to satisfy all my wants. Since I had heard of this legacy I had been doubtful as to my movements. My chance meeting with Francis settled the matter. I resolved at once to leave America, and to return to live in my native country. I knew your address, and wrote to you at once. I trusted that the sight of my old and only friend would console me for the disappointments that life has inflicted on me—and I have not been deceived. At last I have been able to open my heart to a fellow-creature, and relieve myself of the heavy burden which I have borne alone ever since our separation. Now I feel lighter. You are not a severe judge. Doubtless you deplore my weakness, but you do not condemn me. If, as I have already said, I have done no good, neither have I committed any wicked action. I have been a nonentity—an utterly useless being; 'one too many,' like the sad hero of Tourgueneff's sad story. Before leaving, I wrote to Francis informing him that the death of a relative obliged me to return to Europe, and giving him your address, so as not to seem to be running away from him. Then I went on board, and at last reached your home. Dixi!"

Warren, who during this long story had taken care to keep his pipe alight, and had, moreover, nearly drained the bottle of port placed before him, now declared himself ready to listen to his friend's confession. But Hermann had been saddened by all he had heard, and was in no humor for talking. He remarked that it was getting late, and proposed to postpone any further conversation till the morrow.

Warren merely answered, "Very well", knocked the ashes out of his pipe, shared out the remainder of the wine between his host and himself, and, raising his glass, said, in a somewhat solemn tone, "To our youth, Hermann!" After emptying his glass at one draught, he replaced it on the table, and said complacently, "It is long since I have drunk with so much pleasure; for this time I have not drunk to forgetfulness, but to memory."

## II

Warren spent another week in Leipzig with his friend. No man was easier to live with: to every suggestion of Hermann's he invariably answered, "Very well"; and if Hermann proposed nothing, he was quite content to remain seated in a comfortable arm-chair by the fireside, holding a book which he scarcely looked at, and watching the long rolls of smoke from his pipe. He disliked new acquaintances; nevertheless, the friends to whom Hermann introduced him found in him a quiet, unobtrusive, and well-informed companion. He pleased everybody. There was something strange and yet attractive in his person; there was a "charm" about him, people said. Hermann felt the attraction without being able to define in what it consisted. Their former friendship had been renewed unreservedly. The kind of fascination that Warren exercised over all those who approached him often led Hermann to think that it was not unlikely that in his youth he had inspired a real love in Ellen Gilmore.

One evening Hermann took his friend to the theatre, where a comic piece was being performed. In his young days Warren had been very partial to plays of that kind, and his joyous peals of laughter on such occasions still rang in the ears of his friend. But the attempt was a complete failure. Warren watched the performance without showing the slightest interest, and never even smiled. During the opening scenes he listened with attention, as though he were assisting at some performance of the legitimate drama; then, as if he could not understand what was going on before his eyes, he turned away with a wearied air and began looking at the audience. When, at the close of the second act, Hermann proposed that they should leave the house, he answered readily, "Yes, let us go;

all this seems very stupid—we will be much better at home. There is a time for all things, and buffoonery suits me no longer."

There was nothing left in Warren of the friend that Hermann had known fifteen years before. He loved him none the less; on the contrary, to his affection for him had been superadded a feeling of deep compassion. He would have made great sacrifices to secure his friend's happiness, and to see a smile light up the immovable features and the sorrowful dulness of the eye. His friendly anxiety had not been lost upon Warren; and when the latter took his leave, he said with emotion, "You wish me well, my old friend, I see it and feel it; and, believe me, I am grateful. We must not lose sight of each other again—I will write regularly."

A few days later, Hermann received a letter for his friend. It was an American letter, and the envelope was stamped with the initials "E. H." They were those of Ellen Howard, the heroine of Warren's sad history. He forwarded the letter immediately, and wrote at the same time to his friend, "I hope the inclosed brings you good news from America." But in his reply Warren took no notice of this passage, and made no allusion to Ellen. He only spoke of the new house in which he had just settled himself—"to end", as he said, "his days"; and he pressed Hermann to come and join him. The two friends at last agreed to pass Christmas and New Year's Day together; but when December came, Warren urged his friend to hasten his arrival.

"I do not feel well," he wrote, "and I'm often so weary that I stay at home all day. I have made no new acquaintances, and, most likely, will make none. I am alone. Your society would give me great pleasure. Come, your room is ready, and will be, I trust, to your liking. There is a large writing table and tolerably well-filled book-shelves; you can write there quite at your ease, without fear of disturbance. Come as soon as possible, my dear friend. I am expecting you impatiently."

Hermann happened to be at leisure, and was able

to comply with his friend's wish, and to go to him in the first week of December. He found Warren looking worn and depressed. It was in vain he sought to induce him to consult a physician. Warren would reply.

"Doctors can do nothing for my complaint. I know where the shoe pinches. A physician would order me probably to seek relaxation and amusement, just as he would advise a poor devil whose blood is impoverished by bad food to strengthen himself with a generous diet and good wine. The poor man could not afford to get the good living, and I do not know what could enliven or divert me. Travel? I like nothing so well as sitting quietly in my arm-chair. New faces? They would not interest me—yours is the only company I prefer to solitude. Books? I am too old to take pleasure in learning new things, and what I have learned has ceased to interest me. It is not always easy to get what might do one good, and we must take things as they are."

Hermann noticed, as before, that his friend

ate little, but that, on the other hand, he drank a great deal. The sincere friendship he felt for him emboldened him to make a remark on the subject.

"It is true," said Warren, "I drink too much; but what can I do? Food is distasteful to me, and I must keep up my strength somehow. I am in a wretched state; my health is ruined."

One evening, as the two friends were seated together in Warren's room, while the wind and sleet were beating against the window-panes, the invalid began of his own accord to speak about Ellen.

"We now correspond regularly," he said. "She tells me in her last letter that she hopes soon to see me. Do you know, Hermann, that she is becoming an enigma for me? It is very evident that she does not treat me like other people, and I often wonder and ask myself what I am in her eyes? What does she feel towards me? Love? That is inadmissible. Pity, perhaps? This then, is the end of my grand dreams— to be an object of pity? I have just answered her letter to say that I am settled here with the fixed intention of ending my useless existence in quiet and idleness. Do you remember a scene in Henry Heine's 'Reisebilder', when a young student kisses a pretty girl, who lets him have his own way and makes no great resistance, because he has told her, 'I will be gone tomorrow at dawn, and I will never see you again'? The certainty of never seeing a person again gives a man the courage to say things that otherwise he would have kept hidden in the most secret depths of his being. I feel that my life is drawing to a close. Do not say no, my dear friend; my presentiments are certain. I have written it to Ellen. I have told her other things besides. What folly! All I have ever done has been folly or chimera. I end my life logically, in strict accordance with my whole Past, by making my first avowal of love on my deathbed. Is not that as useless a thing as can be?"

Hermann would have wished to know some particulars about this letter; but Warren replied, somewhat vaguely, "If I had a copy of my letter, I would show it to you willingly. You know my whole story, and I would not be ashamed to lay before you my last act of folly. I wrote about a fortnight ago, when I felt sure that death was drawing near. I was in a fever, not from fear—Death gains but little by taking my life—but from a singular species of excitement. I do not remember what were the words I used. Who knows? Perhaps this last product of my brain may have been quite a poetical performance. Never mind! I do not repent of what I have done; I am glad that Ellen should know at last that I have loved her silently and hopelessly. If that is not disinterested, what is?" he added with a bitter smile.

Christmas went by sadly. Warren was now so weak that he could scarcely leave his bed for two or three hours each day. Hermann had taken upon himself to send for a doctor, but this later had scarcely known what to prescribe. Warren was suffering from no special malady; he was dying of exhaustion. Now and then, during a few moments, which became daily more rare and more brief, his vivacity would return; but the shadow of Death was already darkening his mind.

On New Year's Eve he got up very late. "We will welcome in the New Year," he said to Hermann. "I hope it may bring you happiness; I know it will bring me rest." A few minutes before midnight he opened the piano, and played with solemnity, and as if it had been a chorale, a song of Schumann's, entitled "To the Drinking-cup of a Departed Friend". Then, on the first stroke of midnight, he filled two glasses with some old Rhenish wine, and raised his own glass slowly. He was very pale, and his eyes were shining with feverish light. He was in a state of strange and fearful excitement. He looked at the glass which he held, and repeated deliberately a verse of the song which he had just been playing. "The vulgar cannot understand what I see at the bottom of this cup." Then, at one draught, he drained the full glass.

While he was thus speaking and drinking, he had taken no notice of Hermann, who was watching him with consternation. Recovering himself at length, he exclaimed, "Another glass, Hermann! To friendship!" He drained this second glass, like the first, to the very last drop; and then, exhausted by the effort he had made, he sank heavily on a chair. Soon after, Hermann led him, like a sleepy child, to his bed.

During the days that followed, he was unable to leave his room; and the doctor thought it right to warn Hermann that all the symptoms seemed to point to a fatal issue.

On the 8th of January a servant from the hotel in the little neighboring town brought a letter, which, he said, required an immediate answer. The sick man was then lying almost unconscious. Hermann broke the seal without hesitation, and read as follows:

"MY DEAR FRIEND,—A visit to Europe which my father had long planned has at last been undertaken. I did not mention it to you, in order to have the pleasure of surprising you. On reaching this place, I learn that the illness of which you spoke in your last letter has not yet left you. Under these circumstances, I will not venture to present myself

without warning you of my arrival, and making sure
that you are able to receive me. I am here with my
brother, who, like myself, would not come so near
to you without seeing you. My father has gone on
to Paris, where Francis and I will join him in a few
days. ELLEN."

Hermann, after one instant's thought, took up his
hat and dismissed the messenger, saying he would
give the answer himself. At the hotel he sent in his
card, with the words, "From Mr. Warren," and was
immediately ushered into Ellen's presence.

She was alone. Hermann examined her rapidly. He
saw an extremely beautiful woman, whose frank and
fearless eyes were fixed on him with a questioning
look.

Hermann had not frequented the society of women
much, and was usually rather embarrassed in their
presence. But on this occasion he thought only of
his friend, and found no difficulty in explaining the
motive of his visit. He told her his friend was ill—
very ill—dying—and that he had opened the letter

addressed to Warren. Ellen did not answer for some time; she seemed not to have understood what she had heard. After a while her eyes filled with tears, and she asked whether she could see Mr. Warren. On Hermann answering in the affirmative, she further inquired whether her brother might accompany her.

"Two visitors might fatigue the invalid too much," said Hermann, "your brother may come later."

"Are you not afraid that my visit may tire him?"

"I do not think so; it will make him very happy."

Ellen only took a few minutes to put on her hat and cloak, and they started. The short journey was accomplished in silence. When they reached the house, Hermann went in first to see how the dying man was. He was lying in his bed, in the delirium of fever, muttering incoherent sentences. Nevertheless he recognized Hermann, and asked for something to drink. After having allayed his thirst, he closed his eyes, as if to sleep.

"I have brought you a friend," said Hermann, "will you see him?"

"Hermann? He is always welcome."

"No; it is a friend from America."

"From America?...I lived there many years... How desolate and monotonous were the shores I visited!..."

"Will you see your friend?"

"I am carried away by the current of the river. In the distance I see dark and shadowy forms; there are hills full of shade and coolness...but I will never rest there."

Hermann retired noiselessly, and returned almost immediately with Ellen.

Warren, who had taken no notice of him, continued to follow the course of his wandering thoughts.

"The river is drawing near to the sea. Already I can hear the roar of the waves...The banks are beginning to be clothed with verdure...The hills are drawing nearer...It is dark now. Here are the big trees beneath which I have dreamed so often. A radiant apparition shines through their foliage...It comes towards me… Ellen!"

She was standing beside the bed. The dying man saw her, and without showing the least surprise, said with a smile, "Thank God! you have come in time. I knew you were coming."

He murmured a few unintelligible words, and then remained silent for a long while. His eyes were wide open. Suddenly he cried, "Hermann!"

Hermann came and stood beside Ellen.

"The pendulum…You know what I mean?" A frank childish smile—the smile of his student days—lighted up his pallid face. He raised his right hand, and tracing in the air with his forefinger a wide semicircle, to imitate the oscillation of a pendulum, he said, "Then." He then figured in the same manner a more limited and slower movement, and after repeating it several times, said, "Now." Lastly, he pointed straight before him with a motionless and almost menacing finger, and said with a weak voice, "Soon."

He spoke no more, and closed his eyes. The

breathing was becoming very difficult.

Ellen bent, over him, and called him softly, "Henry, Henry!" He opened his eyes. She brought her mouth close to his ear, and said, with a sob, "I have always loved you."

"I knew it from the first," he said, quietly and with confidence.

A gentle expression stole over his countenance, and life seemed to return. Once more he had the confident look of youth. A sad and beautiful smile played on his lips; he took the hand of Ellen in his, and kissed it gently.

"How do you feel now?" inquired Hermann.

The old answer, "Very well."

His hands were plucking at the bedclothes, as if he strove to cover his face with them. Then his arms stiffened and the fingers remained motionless.

"Very well," he repeated.

He appeared to fall into deep thought. There was a long pause. At last he turned a dying look, fraught with tender pity and sadness, towards Ellen, and in a low voice, which was scarcely audible, he said these two words, with a slight emphasis on the first—" PERFECTLY well."

# 一位纽英格兰的尼姑

[美] M.衣·味尔根斯

　　午后也已经是向晚的时候了，光线正在昏暗
下去。外面院子里的树影也变过了样子了。从远
处传来有些乳牛的鸣声和小铃儿的丁零摇振之
音。农场的小车，有时颠摇过去，路上就飞起一
阵灰来。几位穿蓝衬衣的农夫，也肩荷着锄铲，
慢慢儿拖着笨重的脚步走过去了。在暖和的空气
里有小队的飞蝇在行人面前上下地飞翔鸣动。事
事物物之上，仿佛是正只为了将归沉寂的原因而
起了一种幽微的摇动——这实在也正是一种沉静
寂灭和夜色将临的前兆。

　　这一种淡淡的日暮的摇动，也感染到了露衣
莎·霭丽思的身上。她在她的起坐室的窗前和平
沉静地缝她的针线已经缝了一个下半日了。现在
她很小心地把针儿插入了她的正在缝纫的衣服之

中，把这衣服折叠得整整齐齐，更和她的顶针和线球剪刀之类一道安放入了一只手提篮里。露衣莎·霭丽思在她的一生里从没有把这些妇人缝纫用的随身小件乱放遗失过一次，这些随身的用具，因为使用得很久和长不离手的原因，几乎是已经变成了她自己的形体的一部分的样子。

露衣莎在胸前腰际缚上了一条绿色的胸围，取出了一顶周围缀着绿色丽绷的平顶宽边的草帽来。然后拿了一只蓝青的粗窑小碗，她为摘取夜点心的莓果而走到了园中。莓果摘取之后，她就坐下在后门台阶的段上，在那里摘下这莓果的茎来，很小心地把摘下的茎干又收聚在胸围斗里，然后她就把这些不要的茎干丢入了鸡笼。她又向台阶边上的草里深沉看视了一番，看她自己究竟有没有把茎干之类遗掉在那里的草间地上。

露衣莎的行动是很慢很沉静的，为准备一餐夜点心，她不得不费许多的工夫。但当准备好了之后，她却总把它安放得齐齐整整，看起来真仿佛她是她自己的一位尊客的样子。那张小方桌正摆在厨房的中心正中的地面，上面盖着一块浆得硬挺挺的麻纱桌布，桌布边沿上有种种的花形在那里放光。露衣莎有一块蔷薇色的绫巾罩在她的茶盘之上，茶盘里排放着一只满贮茶匙的细纹玻璃杯，一个收盛奶油的长银瓶，一只细瓷的糖碗，一副淡红细瓷的茶托和茶杯。露衣莎每天用的尽是些细致的瓷器——这是她和她的左右近邻们绝对不同的一件事情。邻居们关于这一点也在他们自己的中间在幽私地说长道短。因为他们在平时的饭桌上用都是些平常的粗窑陶器，他们的最好的全副细瓷器具，常宝藏在客厅的食器架上的，而露衣莎·霭丽思也并不见得比他们富裕，并不见得比他们更高一等，可是她却老在用那一种细瓷的食器。她的晚餐的蔬菜，是一满玻璃盆的糖拌的莓果，一碟小圆烧面包和一碟脆白的饼干。还有一两叶卷心洋莴苣菜的菜叶，是经她切得很细致优美的，也摆在那里。露衣莎最喜欢这洋莴苣菜，在她那小小的园里，她是把这菜培养得十分完美的。虽然是很少量很文雅地在吃，可是她却吃得很称心。看她那种吃的样子，觉得一堆颇不少的食物竟会消蚀下去的这件事情，简直是一件奇事。

　　吃完了夜点心之后，她就倒满了一碟烤得

很精致的小圆薄面包，拿着走到了后面的院子里头。

"西撒！"她叫着说，"西撒！西撒！"

院子里听得见一种突冲的声音和一条链子的击响，半隐藏在高茎杂草和花枝中间的一间小小的狗舍门口，就现出了一只大的黄白犬来。露衣莎拍拍它的头，把那碟小圆薄面包给了它吃。于是她就回转到屋里，去细心地洗涤茶器，揩擦细致杯碟去了。黄昏的黑影深了起来；从开在那里的窗口飞进来的蛙唱的声音，异常地响而且锐。忽而一阵尖锐的长响又侵入了窗来，是一只雨蛙的鸣声。露衣莎脱去了她的绿色棉布的胸围。里面露出了一条红白印花的较短的棉纱胸围来。她点上了洋灯，就又坐下去再去缝她的针线。

约莫半点钟之后，爵·达盖脱走向她的屋里来了。她听见他的沉重的脚步在步道上走，就立了起来脱去了那条红白印花的胸围。在这印花胸围之下另外她还有一条穿在那里——是一条下面用细麻纱镶着滚边的白葛布的胸围，这是当她接待客人的时候才服用的东西。若不是有客人在面前，她总是把那条缝纫时用的棉纱胸围罩在这条白葛布的胸围之上的。她用了一丝不乱的急速的手法把那条红白的胸围折叠好，然后又把它收藏在一只桌子的抽斗里面，恰正在这个时候门就开了，爵·达盖脱走了进来。

他一走进来就仿佛是全间屋里都充满了他的行动身体似的打破了这屋里的和平沉静的空气。本来是睡着在南窗前的绿笼里的一只黄而且小的金丝雀惊醒了转来，在笼里不安似的振翻摇动，把它的两只黄小的翅膀死劲地在向笼丝扑打。这小鸟当爵·达盖脱走进这屋里来的时候总没有一次不是这样的。

"请你的晚安。"露衣莎说。她伸出她的手去，仍保持着一种谨严恳笃的态度。

"请你的晚安，露衣莎。"这男子用了粗大的声音回答她。

她替他摆好了一张椅子，两人就隔住了一张桌子而遥遥相对地坐下了。

他挺身坐在那里，把他那双粗重的脚端端正正地伸着，做了一种适意的谨严的态度在看周围屋里的样子。她虽也坐得很直，可是优婉得可怜，把她那双纤手安放在着白葛布的膝上。

"今天真是一天好天气呀。"达盖脱说。

"嗳，天气是真好，"露衣莎柔婉地附和着说。停了一会，她又问他，"你今天在晒干草么？"

"是的，我今天晒了一天的干草，在下面十亩地的大空场里。真是了不得的苦工。"

"可不是么？"

"是啊，是在太阳火里的苦热的工作呀。"

"你母亲今天好么？"

"嗳，母亲是很好的。"

"李丽玳儿现在是在她那里罢？"

达盖脱涨红了脸。"是的，她是，在她那里。"他迟迟地回答了一声。

他的年纪已经是不很轻的了，可是在他的那张大脸上却还映着一种小孩子似的神气。露衣莎的年纪并没有他那么大，她的颜面也要比他的白净光洁些，可是看将起来总觉得她似乎要比他老一点的样子。

"我想她一定是很能帮助你母亲的。"她又继续着说。

"我想她是的。母亲若没有了她，我怕她老

人家将不能够过去哩。"达盖脱说，表示着一种困惑的热情。

"她真是一位很能干的姑娘。并且她也很好看。"露衣莎说。

"是的，她的相儿是很好看的。"

忽而达盖脱弄起摆在桌子上的书本来了。桌上有一本红方的署写姓名的册子和一本少妇的礼赠之书摆在那里，原系属于露衣莎的母亲的东西。他一本一本地拿了起来，打开来看了一下；然后又把它们搁下，把那本署写姓名的册子搁上了那本礼赠之书的高头。

露衣莎含了一种柔婉的不安的样子尽在守视着那两本书。最后她终究站了起来，把书本的位置换过，将那本署写姓名的册子换放成了底下的一本。这是这两本书的本来摆在那里的样子。

达盖脱做了一脸稍觉难受的微笑。"把两本书中间的任何一本摆上了高头，那又有什么关系呢？"他说。

露衣莎含着了一脸请求原谅的微笑看了他一眼。"我可是常是那样地把它们摆着的。"她轻轻地说。

"你对无论什么物事总是那么不惮烦地细心的。"达盖脱又装着笑脸说，他的那张大脸却红涨起来了。

他在那里总又坐了一个钟头的光景，然后立起来要走了。正在走出去的中间，他钩着了一块炉前的粗毯几乎跌了一跤，把身体撑住复回原来的姿势的时候，却又冲着了放在桌上的露衣莎的提篮，终于把它打翻掉到了地上。

他先看看露衣莎，然后又看看在地上滚动的线球之类；就很笨重地把身体伏了倒去想要把它们来捡拾起来，但她却劝阻他可以不必。"不要紧的，"她说，"等你去了之后我会来捡拾起来的。"

她说话的时候略带有一种很不易觉察的偏执的样子。或者她是有一点被搅乱得不自在了，或者也许是他的神经兴奋状态感染了她的缘故，故而使她在竭力想慰抚他要他安心的态度中间露出了一点仿佛是勉强的神情。

爵·达盖脱一走到了外面，便深深地吸了一口甜美的夜间的空气而长叹了一声，并且感到了一种如释重负的感觉，正同一位无邪而满怀好意的粗暴野汉闯大祸而从一家贩卖精细的瓷窑器店里退出来的一样。

一面，在露衣莎的方面呢，也感到了一种同样的感觉，正仿佛同一位善心的着急很久的贩卖瓷器的店主，于那个同野熊似的粗汉退出店后所感到的感觉一样。

她先缚上了那条红白印花的，然后又缚上了那条绿色的胸围，将打翻在地上的各种物事——细心地捡起重把它们放入了原来的手提篮里，更将那块炉前的粗毯铺了一铺平直。她又把洋灯移放到了地板之上，很精细地检视起铺地板的毛绒毯来。她甚至把手指伸出向地板上去擦擦，又举起手指来审视了一回。

"他却踏进了许多灰尘来在这里，"她轻轻地念着说，"我本来就在想他是一定要踏进些来的。"

露衣莎就拿出了一个盛灰的盘和刷子来，很细心地把爵·达盖脱的足印扫了一扫干净。

这事情假若是使他知道了的话，那这又必将增加上些他的困惑与不安无疑，虽然这对于他对她的一片至诚之心原是丝毫也不会有什么影响的。他每礼拜要来看露衣莎·霭丽思两次，而每次来的时候，坐在她的这间收拾得很精雅而又香又软的屋里，他总觉得身体的四面是仿佛被细致的花边篱笆包围住在那里的样子。他真怕敢动一动，免得他的那双粗手粗足要将这同神话里老有的似的细蛛网儿触破，并且他也老觉着露衣莎也在那里很担心地守着他，怕他真的要闯出这样的祸来。

可是不晓怎么的这种细致的花边网和露衣莎总在强迫着要求他的无条件的尊敬与忍耐和忠诚。在他们的中间是已经经过了一个差不多有十五年之久的特异的求婚情事的，现在是在一个月之内就要结婚了。在这十五年中的十四年间他们俩竟没有见到过一次面，并且两人之间在这十四年中就是来往的信件也是交换得很少很少的。爵在这十四年中就一径住在奥斯屈拉利亚，他到这金矿地去本就为想发财而去的，一去他就住下在那里直到他发到了财为止。若说想发到财非要在那里住五十年不可的话，那他也许会在那里住五十年，等到了衰老得连走路都颠摇不定的时候才回来和露衣莎结婚也说不定，或者简直是死掉在那里再也不回来和露衣莎结婚也说不定。

　　但是十四年间财是发到了，而他也为想和在这十四年中间一点儿也不起疑惑只在忍耐地等着他的这个女人结婚的原因回到故乡来了。

　　在他们的定婚之后不久，他就把他的想到这新矿地去的计划，和打算在他们结婚之前弄到一宗相当的财产的决心对露衣莎说了。她听了他的话也仍旧不失她的那种优美的沉着的态度对他表示了同意，这一种优美的沉着的态度是永也不会从她的身边失去的，就是当她的爱人要出发就道去试那个前途不定的很远的旅行的时候，她也仍旧是这样保持着在那里。至于虽则是被他自己的铁样的决心鼓励得很坚固的爵呢，到了最后的一刹那却有点忍不能忍地颓丧起来了，但是露衣莎仍不过是脸上露了一点微红上前去和他亲了个嘴，好好地和他诀别。

　　"总之这是不要几年的。"可怜的爵压住了情热嗄声地说。但是这一个"不要几年"却成了十四个年头。

　　在这一个时期之内有许多出乎意料的事情发生了。露衣莎的母亲和哥哥都死了，她在这世上就只剩了孤零零的一个，但是在这些事情中间的最大的一件却是一件微妙渐进的事情，是天性纯朴的他们俩所不能了解的——就是露衣莎的性情趣向走上了另一条路的这事情，这一条路呀，在平静的天地之间原是平坦的一条直道，可是只是直而不曲，一直要到了她的坟墓中间才告终结的一条道路，而且又是很狭，在这一条路上连容一个旁人在她边上的这点余裕都不能够有的。

当爵·达盖脱回来的时候（他是不曾把要回来的事情通知她的）露衣莎最初所感到的是一种惊愕之情，这在她对她自己虽则是不肯承认，而他也是再也梦想不到的事情，但这却是真情。在十五年之前她是的确对他发生过爱情的——至少她想她自己是这样的。正在那个时候，柔和地顺从追随着少女期的自然的春情，她是把将来的结婚这件事情当作一个合理的解决与人生的或然的愿望看的。她只以沉静的柔顺听取了她母亲对于这问题的意见。她的母亲是以富有冷静的理性与优美和平的气质见称的人。当爵·达盖脱来求婚的时候她母亲也曾很贤明地和她仔细讲过，所以露衣莎便毫无踌躇地接受了他。他实在是她的开情窦以来的第一个爱人。

她在这样长年的岁月中间对他是再忠诚也没有的了。对于去和另外一个人结婚的这一个想头，就是在梦里她也不曾梦到过。她的生活，尤其是最近的七年间的生活，老是充满着愉快的和平的色彩，对于她的爱人的远离异域她从来还没有感到过不满或难耐的心情，可是她却也老在打算着他的回来而在把两人将来的结婚当作一件事理的必不可免的结果看。但是呀，不晓怎么的她终于变成了一种奇怪的想法，把这一件结婚的事情总看作了将来很远很远的事实，由她看来，仿佛这件事情是非要到今生完毕他生开始的边际到来的时候不会实现的样子。

在十四年间她所盼望着，期待着和他结婚的爵现在如她所盼望着的回来的时候，她倒同从来也没有想到过这事情的人一样变得惊愕仓皇惘然不知所措了。

至于爵的惊惧震愕呢，在时间上比她的还要来得落后一点。他看看露衣莎，一看就觉得他旧日的那种赞美之情的确还有维护的价值。她比从前真没有变过什么。她仍复还保有着那种美丽的风度和温柔的雅致，而她的一举一动一丝一发，他以为还是同从前一样的富有牵引力的，在他自己的一方面呢，他的应做的事情是已经做了，他已可以不再去孜孜于求利求财了，而旧日的那种寻奇猎美之风仍旧和往日一样的甜蜜、一样的明朗，在他的耳朵里吁吁地吹啸。他在过去在这些风声里听惯的歌声原是露衣莎这一个名字。他直到现在也已经有好久好久还很忠诚地确信着他所听见的仍旧是这一个名字，但到了最后他觉得虽则风声里所唱着的歌总仍旧还是这一个，可是歌声里的人名却有了一个另外的名字了，而在露衣莎的一面呢，觉得这风声从没有比幽幽的微鸣更响一点过。现在可是连这微鸣都衰杀下去了，一切的事物都已经变成了静默。她半用意识似的静听了一忽儿，然后又很平静地转过了身仍复去缝她自己的嫁衣裳去了。

　　爵已经把他自己的房子规模很大很华壮地施了一番修改了。这当然仍旧是他那间旧日的农场里的老家，新婚的他们夫妇也非在那里住下去不可，因为爵不愿意抛弃他的老母，她老人家是不肯离去这一间她的老屋的。所以露衣莎就非离去了她自己的那间房子而去和他们同住不行，每天早晨，起床之后在她的那些整洁的处女时代的器具什物及娘家的一切所有物的中间走来走去走走的当儿，她看来看去总感觉得仿佛是一个人对于自己的亲爱者们的面孔以后怕将看不见了的样子。当然在一定的限度之内她原可以把这些物事带一部分去的，可是呀，把它们的旧日的情形位置变换之后，那它们简直要不是本来的它们一样地变成一种新样子的。并且此外还有许多在她的这个满足而清静的生活里的特异之处，她大约也非全部舍去了不可。以后比这些娴雅过细的日课更要辛苦的操作，大约也总要丛集上她的身来。一间很大的房子不得不整理；朋友来往的交际不得不应酬；爵的严肃衰弱的老母不得不侍奉；而且农村里的节俭之风是很盛行的，她若用一个以上的使女的时候，恐怕又要违反这一乡的习俗。露衣莎在家里有一个小蒸馏器备在那里的，当夏天的节季她老爱把玫瑰，薄荷香草等的芳甘的花露蒸馏出来。但不久之后这蒸馏器也不得不高搁起来了。她的各种花露水原也已经积贮得很多了，可是此后单就为了蒸馏的快乐而去蒸馏的余

闲总也要没有了罢。因为否则爵的母亲怕要以这
事情为痴傻而笑她，她老人家对这事情况且已经
讽示过意见了。露衣莎最喜欢把麻纱布类缝接拢
来，并不常是因为有缝接的必要，她不过单是想
享受享受在这中间的单纯柔雅的乐趣而已。只因
为想享受享受这重把它们缝接拢来的快乐之故，
她曾经几度地把已经缝好的接缝拆开来过了，这
事情说出来大约她是总不乐意承认的，可是事实
上她却老在那里干这一个玩意儿。在甘美日长的
午后，坐在窗前，幽幽雅雅地把针头向纤细的织
缝里穿缝过去的她，看起来实在好像是一位象征
和平清静这一种情调的女神。但是在将来像这一
种说起来原也可笑的寻求快乐的机会大约总也很
少了罢。爵的母亲，这一位就是到了老年也专喜
欢管人闲事生性不驯的老主妇，或者也竟许是具
有烈烈轰轰的男性的粗鲁气质的爵他自己，对这
些优美而无意思的老处女式的行为，大约总也要
皱起眉头笑着出来劝阻的罢。

　　露衣莎对于她那间孤寂的住屋的整理与收
拾，几乎抱有一种艺术家的热狂的样子。她看了
被她揩擦得亮晶晶同珠玉似的放光的玻璃窗，心

里头就会感到一种真正的得意的动悸。对她的整理得清清洁洁，里面的物什件件都折叠得好好，秩序整然而且带有些防虫紫菊花三叶香草和清洁这一件事情本身的气息的箱笼抽斗之类，闲雅地看看，她觉得看一辈子也不会看厌。以后光就是这一件事情还能够这样地存续下去不能，她也觉得很没有把握。她常有许多预想将来的可怕的幻觉，因为太可怕了，一半她却不得不自责自己的无礼猥亵而努力地在把这些幻觉排除开去，这些幻觉不外乎粗野的男子用的物什，这儿一堆那儿一簇地周围散放着的杂乱情形，和因为一个粗野的男子处在其中的缘故，在幽静雅洁保持着融合的色彩的环境之中必然要起来的那一种灰尘龌龊与凌乱的样子。

在她的种种不安的预感之中，还有一件并不能说不重大的，是关于西撒的事情。西撒在狗的中间实在可说是一只被幽闭在那里的禁犬。在它的一生中的大部分它只住在那间不与外界往来的狗舍里过去的，同它的同类的交游当然是断绝了的不必提起，就是各种无邪的狗类的娱乐它也一点也不曾有过。西撒从它的幼年初期以来从来也没有过上一只小白兔的洞穴边去静候捕捉一次的事情；上邻家的厨房门口去拖一块被抛出来的骨头来吃的快乐经验它也从来没有过的。这都因为当它还没有脱出小狗时期的时候犯下了一次罪的缘故。这一只相貌也很柔和，全体的样子也并不邪恶的老犬，对这一次罪恶的悔恨之情，究竟能有几许的深刻，那是谁也不能够知道；不过不管它究竟有没有生到悔恨，总之它却受到了十足的刑法的谴责了。老西撒在怒吠狂叫里举起声来的事情是很少有的；它身体长得很肥，老在做打盹想睡的样子；它的蒙胧的老眼边上有两个黄色的圈纹看起来像煞是它戴在那里的眼镜；但是在一位它的邻人的手上却印着有几个西撒的雪白锋利的幼齿之纹在那里，因此它就不得不被系在一条链子的一头，孤孤单单地在这一间小舍里过它十四年间的独居生活了。被咬的这位邻人因为伤处的剧痛与怒恼的结果，要求或者将西撒来击毙或者将它完全放逐出去。所以狗的属主的露衣莎的哥哥就替它造成了一间狗舍把它吊系了进去，这已经是十四年前的事情了，在它的幼年活泼的浓兴之中它犯下了那一口可纪念的毒咬，以后除了在它的主人或露衣莎的严重监视之下以链子的一头为度，试过几次短短的游行之外，这一只老狗就完全变成了一个监狱里的囚犯了。

本来就没有多大野心的它对于这件事情究竟是否在感到无上的荣耀的，却是一个疑问，但是事实上它的身上居然也因此而担负着有一点不值钱的名誉。村里的许多大人和一般的小孩都在把它当作了一只狞猛的野兽在看。从恶名声的方面说来，怕露衣莎·霭丽思的这只老黄狗的名声并不在被圣乔治所屠斩的那条毒龙的名声之下的。母亲们老在用了严重的叮嘱告诫她们的子女，教大家都不要太走近这一只狗的身边，小孩们听了自然最乐意相信，被一种恐怖的快乐所迷引，他们于轻脚轻手地偷跑过露衣莎的房子的时候，对这一只可怕的老犬总不免抛几眼偷视或回头来看它一阵。假若偶然间它做一声嘎声的怒吼，那周围就要起大恐怖了。行路的旅人偶尔到露衣莎的院子里来的，总满怀了敬意对它看看，并且要寻问一声那链子究竟是坚牢的不是。西撒假如是照寻常的样子被放着的时候，那它也不过是一只极平常的狗罢了，绝不会引起人家的什么注意解释的，但是一被链子来锁起，它的恶名就加上了声势到它的身上，而它自己的本来面目也就因而失掉，看起来就变得阴暗朦胧异常的硕大了。不过有宽大的理性和粗暴的气质的爵·达盖脱对它却还能看出它的本来的面目来。他毫不会把露衣莎的婉转的警告摆在心上，敢大胆地直走上它的身边，去拍拍它的头，或者竟想试放它出来恢复它的自由。但因为露衣莎惊骇得太厉害了他才不敢下手，不过关于这事情他在这中间却总时时在很坚决地宣述他的意见。"在这镇上怕再也没有一只比它性情更好的狗了，"他总是这样地在说，"把它像那样的在那儿系锁起来实在是一件很残酷的事情。将来总有一天我要把它释放出来。"

将来她们的财产所有不得不完全并合在一起的时候，露衣莎怕他总有一天要实行这计划的。她一个人会想象起西撒在这一个清静而无守备的村子里头乱暴狂跳的样子来，她在想象里看见无辜的小孩们在路上遇着了它被它咬得血涔涔滴了。她自身呢，对这只老狗原是非常之痛爱的，因为它是属于她已死的哥哥的遗物，而它对她也老是很柔顺驯服的。但是她对于它的那种狞恶的野性，仍旧是抱有绝大的恐怖，坚信它是不会失去的。她老在告诫人家，教他们不要太走近它的身边去。她喂它的时候用的总是些玉蜀黍粉糊与小薄烧面包等制欲的食料，绝不用那些由肉类与骨头弄成的有刺激与残忍性的食品去激起它的危险野性来的。露衣莎守视着这老狗在咀嚼它那份单纯的食料，一边想起了她自己的就要到来的婚期，竟不觉惊愕了起来身体上起了颤栗。可是将代那种香甜的和平融洽的情调而起的乱杂与纷扰的预感，西撒的狂乱怒闯的兆头，与她那只小黄金丝雀的乱扑乱跳的事实等都不能给她以一点稍有变换的口实。爵·达盖脱却从来是就爱她的，他为了她并且是去苦劳了这些个年头了。不管它将来事情要变得怎么样，在她的一方面，总不能对他变作不忠不实而使他伤心失望的。她只在很优美地一针一针地细缝她的嫁时衣类，时间已经过去了，直到了去她的婚期只有一礼拜的日期之前。那是一天礼拜二的晚上，她们的婚期原是定在下礼拜三的日里的。

那是一天满月之夜的晚上。差不多九点钟的时候，露衣莎从村道上向下散了一程步。村道两旁都是成熟的稻田，是以矮矮的石墙做界的。石墙之旁生长着些丰盛的矮树之丛，中间也杂有些野樱桃老苹果等很高的杂树在那里。不多一忽儿露衣莎在石墙上坐下了，含了一种微微的悲哀沉思之情在向左右前后眺望。高高的乌果树丛与金莲花薮和悬钩子藤刀豆枝等结合交连在一处把她四边围住了。她在这些枝藤矮树之间占得了小小的一席空地。在村道的一面和她相对的一方，是一排延长的树列。月亮射在这些树枝的中间。树叶闪烁，都反射出了一层银色的光辉。路上在那里交互闪动的是美丽的银色和黑影相交的斑点。空气里充满着一种神秘的蜜腻香甜。"这难道是野葡萄么？"露衣莎轻轻地自对自地说。她在那里坐了好久的一会。正想立起来走的时候，她却听见了些脚步声音和轻轻的谈话之声。于是她就不得不静止着不动了。这本来是一个僻静的地方，她倒有点觉得胆小起来了。她想她应该在树影里静静地躲着，让这几个人，不管他们是谁，从她那里走过去才行。

　　但是当他们正要走到而还没有到她那里的时候，话声停止了，脚步声也同时不再听得出来。

她才知道这些话声脚步声的主人也在石墙上坐下了。她正在想或者她可以不被他们觉察而轻轻地偷跑开他们，但正在这个时候话声又把静默打破了。这是爵·达盖脱的声音。她就静静地坐在那里听着。

说话开始之前先来了一声高声的叹息，这叹声同说话的声音一样是她所听惯的音调。"噢，"达盖脱说，"那么，我想，你总已经下了决心了罢？"

"是的，"另外的一种声音说，"我想到了后天就走。"

"那是李丽玳儿的声音。"露衣莎自己一个人在想。这话声连它的主人的形体都在她的心里唤醒过来了。她看见了一个高高的，身体长得很丰满的女孩，颜面是很有决心很细白的，在月光里看起来更觉得坚决更觉得洁白了，她的很浓厚的一头金发是编成一个紧紧的结拖在后面的。是一个满保着那种乡间女子特有的镇静强壮和丰润的女孩，她那种机灵的样子就是在一位公主的身上也是很配的。李丽玳儿是为村中大家所崇拜的一个宠儿，她却巧正具备着那种可以挑动人家的赞美的特质。她是一个又善良又美丽又聪明的女子。露衣莎听见人家赞美她的话语也已经不只一次两次了。

"嗳，"达盖脱说，"我也没有一句什么话好说。"

"我也不晓得你将怎么说。"李丽玳儿回答他说。

"真也没有一句话可以说的。"达盖脱重复着说，把话声沉重地拖得很长。于是就来了片时的沉默。"我想那也是很好的，我并没有什么悔恨之情，"到了最后他又开始说，"就是昨天居然那么地说出了——总之，无论如何我们是把我们中间互相感到的感情说出了。我想这是我们大家都明明知道的。当然我是没有法子把事情少许变动一点的。我不得不就这样下去，到下礼拜就和她去结婚。我哪能够把一个已经等了我十四年的女人舍去，而使她伤心失望的呢。"

"假如你明天要这样的薄情欺她的话，那我就不要你了。"那女孩忽然含了热情大胆地辩护着说。

"嗳，当然我不会这样的，给你这一个不要

我的机会的，"他说，"不过我也不相信你真会不
要我的。"

"你瞧着我可真会的。男子汉大丈夫，名誉
正义哪能够不顾着的呢。假如有一位男子为了我
或另外无论哪一个女孩而把这些名誉正义都弃抛
了的话，那我将一点也瞧他不起哩。爵·达盖脱，
你瞧着罢，往后你才知道我的厉害。"

"嗳，你马上就可以看到，我将不为了你或
另外无论哪一个女孩，而把名誉正义等全都置之
于度外。"他回答说。他们俩的话声，简直仿佛
是两人各含了怒气互相在那里争论答辩的样子。
露衣莎尖起了耳朵在听着。

"你觉得你非走不可的这一件事情我是很在
替你痛心的，"爵说，"不过我也想不出法子，或
者这是最善的一法罢。"

"这当然是最善的一法。我希望你和我都能
够有充分的常识才行。"

"嗳，我想你倒是不错的。"爵的声音忽而变
了一种柔和慰抚的低调。"喂，李丽，"他说，"我
是总可以马虎过去的，但我真不忍想到——你总
不至于为此而烦闷伤心罢？"

"我想你总不至于看到我将为了一个已和他人结过婚的男子而烦闷伤心。"

"嗳，我真希望你能如此，——李丽，我真希望你能如此。我的心只有上帝知道。并且——我希望——将来你总有一天——或者你会——遇到一个另外的人——"

"我想我也没有必不会的理由。"忽而她的话声调子变了。以后她就用了一种甘美清澈的声音，说得格外地响，就连在大道之外都可以听到她的话声。"不，爵·达盖脱，"她说，"我这一生中是再也不想和另外一个人结婚了。我是有彻底的常识的，我哪会故意去摧断我自己的肝肠忍心去做一个大傻瓜呢；我可是再也不想结婚了，这一点可以保证你的。我并不是那样的女子，可以把这事情重来一遍的。"

露衣莎在矮树丛的背后听到了一声深沉的感叹和一种温软的动摇。然后李丽又开始说——这声音听起来仿佛是她已经立起来在那里的样子。"这下回可不能再来的了，非加以制止不行，"她说，"我们在这里耽搁得也太久了，回去罢。"

露衣莎在那里坐着呆住了，一边却在听着他

们走回去的脚步声音。停了一会她也站了起来轻
轻地溜回了家中。第二天她把家里的事情仍旧很
有秩序地做了，这是同呼吸一样地有一定的程序
的事情，但是嫁时穿着的衣裳她却不再缝了。她
坐在窗边尽在那里沉思默想，到晚上爵又来了。
露衣莎·霭丽思从来不晓得她自己是有应付事
情的外交手段的，但那一天晚上正要用它的时
候，她却也居然自己在她的仅少的女性的自卫武
器之中发现了，虽则这原不过是一种性质很柔和
的武器。就是到了现在她也几乎不能自信她所听
到的是真的不错的，她还在疑惑不决，假如她把
她的婚约解除的时候究竟会不会给爵一个很大的
打击，她非要暂时把她自己的关于这事情的意思
隐瞒一下，先来探探他的意思看不可。她的这外
交术居然成功了，最后他们俩竟达到了互相了解
的程度。不过这也不是一件容易的事情，因为他
也和她一样地在害怕，生怕他自己的心迹要破露
出来。

她并不提起李丽玳儿的名字。她单只是说，
她对他也并没有一点不满意的地方，不过她像这
样一个人已经住得很久了，真怕把她的这一个生

活样式来改变一下。

"嗳，露衣莎，我是绝不怕的，"达盖脱说。"我若老老实实地说，那我想或者这样倒也比较的好些，不过假如你若愿意守约嫁我的话，那我到死为止绝不会有二意的。我想这一点你总明白的罢。"

"是的，我是明白的。"她说。

那一天晚上她和爵分手的时候觉得比在往日还要恩爱，她们俩有好久好久不曾感到这样的温存慰帖过了。两人各握着手，立在门口悲哀的记忆的最后一阵大浪各打动了他们俩人的衷心。

"嗳，这却不像诸事已经终了的样子如我们所想的一样，露衣莎，是不是？"爵说。

她只摇了摇她的头，在她的沉静的脸上却露现了一阵小小的痉挛。

"我若能帮助你替你做些事情的地方，尽管请你来叫我，"他说，"我是永也不会忘记你的，露衣莎。"于是他就和她亲了一个嘴，沿着村道走下去了。

露衣莎，在那一天晚上只剩了她孤零零一个人的时候，也稍稍流了一阵眼泪，她却不晓得究竟是为了什么。但到了第二天的早晨，当醒转来的时候，她觉得自己正同一位怕把江山失掉的女皇得到了确实的保证的时候一样。

现在是高茎的杂草可以尽管在西撒的那间幽居的小舍周围丛生起来，雪也可以继续不断地落上它的这间小舍的屋顶上来，而它却绝不会到无守备的村子里去狂暴作乱了。现在那个小金丝雀夜夜可以尽管由它去滚成一个和平的小黄圆毯而安眠，不致被恐怖惊醒转来而将它的翅膀打扑上笼丝去了。露衣莎可以由她己心之所欲，尽量地去缝接麻纱，蒸馏蔷薇，打扫揩擦与整整齐齐地折叠衣类去了。那一天下午她在窗前缝着针线，觉得完全是沉浸在和平的空气里的样子。高高的，挺直的，艳丽的李丽玳儿从窗前走了过去；可是露衣莎却一点也没有感到难受。即使说露衣莎·霭丽思在不晓得的中间因图一时的安逸而将她的永久的权利卖去了的话，那也是无伤的，这一时的安逸的滋味实在是鲜美得很，并且到如今为止在这样长的岁月里，这实在是她的唯一的慰安满足的源泉。和平的静肃与狭隘的安宁在她实在是同永久的权利一样地适合的。她邈想着一长

列的未来的日子，看到了这些日子都是圆滑无疵
纯洁得同一串念佛珠上的珠子一样，每一天总同
其他的日子相像，她的心中就不觉充满了感谢之
情而高涨了起来。屋外头是炎热的夏天的午后，
空气里散满着繁忙的收获期里的人和鸟与蜜蜂的
声音，有喂喂的叫声，有金属器具冲击的声音，
有甜蜜的嘤嘤鸟鸣之声，有冗长的蜜蜂的哼声。
露衣莎坐在那里，心里头满贮着祈祷的时候的虔
敬之念在细数她的未来的日子，真像是一位不入
庵院的清静的尼姑。

\* \* \* \* \* \*

上面译出的美国 Mary E.Wilkins 女士的一篇小
说 *A New England Nun*，系由纽约 Harper&Brothers
书店出版的小说集 *A New England Nun and Other
Stories* 里译出来的。原作者味尔根斯女士于
一八六二年生在 Massachusetts 的 Randolph，家
里是一个严守着 Puritanism 的清教徒的家庭，年
纪很轻的时候曾被携至 Vermont，到了女学校卒
业之后，又重回到了兰道儿夫来。一九〇二年和

Dr. Freeman 结了婚，以后就在 New Jersey 住下了。一八八六年印行了她第一本的短篇小说集，嗣后就有许多长短篇的小说创作出来。她善于描写纽英格兰人的顽固的性格，美国的一位批评家 William Lyon Phelps 甚至比她为查、高尔基，说她描写下层工农的情状性格，要比上举两大家更来得合理逼真。少年批评家 Carl Van Doren 也说她是美国 Local fiction 的代表者，加以无限的赞许。我也觉得她的这一种纤纤的格调楚楚的风姿，是为一般男作家所追赶不上的。译文冗赘，把原作的那种纯朴简洁的文体之美完全失去了。并且浅薄轻率的译者，对原文总不免有解错的地方，这一点要请高明的读者赐以指教才行。

还有原文里的几个名字，因为译者读不清楚，所以仍将它们写出在下面。

女主人公 Louisa Ellis

男主人公 Joe Dagget

还有一位女人 Lily Dyer

狗 Caesar

圣乔治的毒龙 St. Georg's Dragon

最后原作者弗丽曼夫人的其他的著作的重

要者，顺便也举两篇在这里：

*A humble romance and other stories.*

*Silence and other stories.*

*Pembroke.*

*The Portion of labor.*

*The shoulder of Atlas.etc.*

一九二九年三月

# A New England Nun

by Mary E.Wilkins Freeman

*I*t was late in the afternoon, and the light was waning. There was a difference in the look of the tree shadows out in the yard. Somewhere in the distance cows were lowing and a little bell was tinkling; now and then a farm-wagon tilted by, and the dust flew; some blue-shirted laborers with shovels over their shoulders plodded past; little swarms of flies were dancing up and down before the peoples' faces in the soft air. There seemed to be a gentle stir arising over everything for the mere sake of subsidence—a very premonition of rest and hush and night.

This soft diurnal commotion was over Louisa Ellis also. She had been peacefully sewing at her sitting-room window all the afternoon. Now she quilted her needle carefully into her work, which she folded precisely, and laid in a basket with her thimble and thread and scissors. Louisa Ellis could not remember that ever in her life she had mislaid one of these little feminine appurtenances, which had become, from long use and constant association, a very part of her personality.

Louisa tied a green apron round her waist, and got out a flat straw hat with a green ribbon. Then she went into the garden with a little blue crockery bowl, to pick some currants for her tea. After the currants were picked she sat on the back door-step and stemmed them, collecting the stems carefully in her apron, and afterwards throwing them into the hen-coop. She looked sharply at the grass beside the step to see if any had fallen there.

Louisa was slow and still in her movements; it took her a long time to prepare her tea; but when ready it was set forth with as much grace as if she had been a veritable guest to her own self. The little square table stood exactly in the centre of the kitchen, and was covered with a starched linen cloth whose border pattern of flowers glistened. Louisa had a damask napkin on her tea-tray, where were arranged a cut-glass tumbler full of teaspoons, a silver cream-pitcher, a china sugar-bowl, and one pink china cup and saucer. Louisa used china every day — something which none of her neighbors did. They whispered about it among themselves. Their daily tables were laid with common crockery, their sets of best china stayed in the parlor closet, and Louisa Ellis was no richer nor better bred than they. Still she would use the china. She had for her supper a glass dish full of sugared currants, a plate of little cakes, and one of light white biscuits. Also a leaf or two of lettuce, which she cut up daintily. Louisa was very fond of lettuce, which she raised to perfection in her little garden. She ate quite heartily, though in a delicate, pecking way; it seemed almost surprising that any considerable bulk of the food should vanish.

After tea she filled a plate with nicely baked thin

corn-cakes, and carried them out into the back-yard.

"Ceasar!" she called. "Ceasar! Ceasar!"

There was a little rush, and the clank of a chain, and a large yellow-and-white dog appeared at the door of his tiny hut, which was half hidden among the tall grasses and flowers. Louisa patted him and gave him the corn-cakes. Then she returned to the house and washed the tea-things, polishing the china carefully. The twilight had deepened; the chorus of the frogs floated in at the open window wonderfully loud and shrill, and once in a while a long sharp drone from a tree-toad pierced it. Louisa took off her green gingham apron, disclosing a shorter one of pink and white print. She lighted her lamp, and sat down again with her sewing.

In about half an hour Joe Dagget came. She heard his heavy step on the walk, and rose and took off her pink-and-white apron. Under that was still another — white linen with a little cambric edging on the bottom; that was Louisa's company apron. She never wore it without her calico sewing apron over it unless she had a guest. She had barely folded the pink and white one with methodical haste and laid it in a table-drawer when the door opened and Joe Dagget entered.

He seemed to fill up the whole room. A little yellow canary that had been asleep in his green cage at the south window woke up and fluttered wildly, beating his little yellow wings against the wires. He always did so when Joe Dagget came into the room.

"Good evening," said Louisa. She extended her hand with a kind of solemn cordiality.

"Good evening, Louisa," returned the man, in a loud voice.

She placed a chair for him, and they sat facing each other, with the table between them. He sat bolt-upright, toeing out his heavy feet squarely, glancing with a good-humored uneasiness around the room. She sat gently erect, folding her slender hands in her white-linen lap.

"Been a pleasant day," remarked Dagget.

"Real pleasant," Louisa assented, softly. "Have

you been haying?" she asked, after a little while.

"Yes, I've been haying all day, down in the ten-acre lot. Pretty hot work."

"It must be."

"Yes, it's pretty hot work in the sun."

"Is your mother well to-day?"

"Yes, mother's pretty well."

"I suppose Lily Dyer's with her now?"

Dagget colored. "Yes, she's with her," he answered, slowly.

He was not very young, but there was a boyish look about his large face. Louisa was not quite as old as he, her face was fairer and smoother, but she gave people the impression of being older.

"I suppose she's a good deal of help to your mother," she said, further.

"I guess she is; I don't know how mother'd get along without her," said Dagget, with a sort of embarrassed warmth.

"She looks like a real capable girl. She's pretty-looking too," remarked Louisa.

"Yes, she is pretty fair looking."

Presently Dagget began fingering the books on the table. There was a square red autograph album, and a Young Lady's Gift-Book which had belonged to Louisa's mother. He took them up one after the other and opened them; then laid them down again, the album on the Gift-Book.

Louisa kept eying them with mild uneasiness. Finally she rose and changed the position of the books, putting the album underneath. That was the way they had been arranged in the first place.

Dagget gave an awkward little laugh. "Now what difference did it make which book was on top?" said he.

Louisa looked at him with a deprecating smile. "I always keep them that way," murmured she.

"You do beat everything," said Dagget, trying to laugh again. His large face was flushed.

He remained about an hour longer, then rose to take leave. Going out, he stumbled over a rug, and trying to recover himself, hit Louisa's work-basket on the table, and knocked it on the floor.

He looked at Louisa, then at the rolling spools; he ducked himself awkwardly toward them, but she stopped him. "Never mind," said she, "I'll pick them up after you're gone."

She spoke with a mild stiffness. Either she was a little disturbed, or his nervousness affected her, and made her seem constrained in her effort to reassure him.

When Joe Dagget was outside he drew in the sweet evening air with a sigh, and felt much as an innocent and perfectly well-intentioned bear might after his exit from a china shop.

Louisa, on her part, felt much as the kind-hearted, long-suffering owner of the china shop might have done after the exit of the bear.

She tied on the pink, then the green apron, picked up all the scattered treasures and replaced them in her work-basket, and straightened the rug. Then she set the lamp on the floor, and began sharply examining the carpet. She even rubbed her fingers over it, and looked at them.

"He's tracked in a good deal of dust," she murmured. "I thought he must have."

Louisa got a dust-pan and brush, and swept Joe Dagget's track carefully.

If he could have known it, it would have increased his perplexity and uneasiness, although it would not have disturbed his loyalty in the least. He came twice a week to see Louisa Ellis, and every time, sitting there in her delicately sweet room, he felt as if surrounded by a hedge of lace. He was afraid to stir lest he should put a clumsy foot or hand through the fairy web, and he had always the consciousness that Louisa was watching fearfully lest he should.

Still the lace and Louisa commanded perforce his perfect respect and patience and loyalty. They were to be married in a month, after a singular courtship which had lasted for a matter of fifteen years. For fourteen out of the fifteen years the two had not once seen each other, and they had seldom exchanged letters. Joe had been all those years in Australia, where he had gone to make his fortune, and where he had stayed until he made it. He would have stayed fifty years if it had taken so long, and come home feeble and tottering, or never come home at all, to marry Louisa.

But the fortune had been made in the fourteen years, and he had come home now to marry the woman who had been patiently and unquestioningly waiting for him all that time.

Shortly after they were engaged he had announced to Louisa his determination to strike out into new fields, and secure a competency before they should be married. She had listened and assented with the sweet serenity which never failed her, not even when her lover set forth on that long and uncertain journey. Joe, buoyed up as he was by his sturdy determination, broke down a little at the last, but Louisa kissed him with a mild blush, and said good-bye.

"It won't be for long," poor Joe had said, huskily; but it was for fourteen years.

In that length of time much had happened. Louisa's mother and brother had died, and she was all alone in the world. But greatest happening of all — a subtle happening which both were too simple to understand — Louisa's feet had turned into a path, smooth maybe under a calm, serene sky, but so straight and unswerving that it could only meet a check at her grave, and so narrow that there was no room for any one at her side.

Louisa's first emotion when Joe Dagget came home (he had not apprised her of his coming) was consternation, although she would not admit it to herself, and he never dreamed of it. Fifteen years ago she had been in love with him — at least she considered herself to be. Just at that time, gently acquiescing with and falling into the natural drift of girlhood, she had seen marriage ahead as a reasonable feature and a probable desirability of life. She had listened with calm docility to her mother's views upon the subject. Her mother was remarkable for her cool sense and sweet, even temperament.

She talked wisely to her daughter when Joe Dagget presented himself, and Louisa accepted him with no hesitation. He was the first lover she had ever had.

She had been faithful to him all these years. She had never dreamed of the possibility of marrying any one else. Her life, especially for the last seven years, had been full of a pleasant peace, she had never felt discontented nor impatient over her lover's absence; still she had always looked forward to his return and their marriage as the inevitable conclusion of things. However, she had fallen into a way of placing it so far in the future that it was almost equal to placing it over the boundaries of another life.

When Joe came she had been expecting him, and expecting to be married for fourteen years, but she was as much surprised and taken aback as if she had never thought of it.

Joe's consternation came later. He eyed Louisa with an instant confirmation of his old admiration. She had changed but little. She still kept her pretty manner and soft grace, and was, he considered, every whit as attractive as ever. As for himself, his stent was done; he had turned his face away from fortune-seeking, and the old winds of romance whistled as loud and sweet as ever through his ears. All the song which he had been wont to hear in them was Louisa; he had for a long time a loyal belief that he heard it still, but finally it seemed to him that although the winds sang always that one song, it had another name. But for Louisa the wind had never more than murmured; now it had gone down, and everything was still. She listened for a little while with half-wistful attention; then she turned quietly away and went to work on her wedding clothes.

Joe had made some extensive and quite magnificent alterations in his house. It was the old homestead; the newly-married couple would live there, for Joe could not desert his mother, who refused to leave her old home. So Louisa must leave hers. Every morning, rising and going about among her neat maidenly possessions, she felt as one looking her last upon the faces of dear friends.

It was true that in a measure she could take them with her, but, robbed of their old environments, they would appear in such new guises that they would almost cease to be themselves. Then there were some peculiar features of her happy solitary life which she would probably be obliged to relinquish altogether. Sterner tasks than these graceful but half-needless ones would probably devolve upon her. There would be a large house to care for; there would be company to entertain; there would be Joe's rigorous and feeble old mother to wait upon; and it would be contrary to all thrifty village traditions for her to keep more than one servant. Louisa had a little still, and she used to occupy herself pleasantly in summer weather with distilling the sweet and aromatic essences from roses and peppermint and spearmint. By-and-by her still must be laid away. Her store of essences was already considerable, and there would be no time for her to distil for the mere pleasure of it. Then Joe's mother would think it foolishness; she had already hinted her opinion in the matter. Louisa dearly loved to sew a linen seam, not always for use, but for the simple, mild pleasure which she took in it. She would have been loath to confess how more than once she had ripped a seam for the mere delight of sewing it together again. Sitting at her window during long sweet afternoons, drawing her needle gently through the dainty fabric, she was peace itself. But there was small chance of such foolish comfort in the future. Joe's mother, domineering, shrewd old matron that she was even in her old age, and very likely even Joe himself, with his honest masculine rudeness, would laugh and frown down all these pretty but senseless old maiden ways.

Louisa had almost the enthusiasm of an artist over the mere order and cleanliness of her solitary home. She had throbs of genuine triumph at the sight of the window-panes which she had polished until they shone like jewels. She gloated gently over her orderly bureau-drawers, with their exquisitely folded contents redolent with lavender and sweet clover and very purity. Could she be sure of the endurance of even this? She had visions, so startling that she half repudiated them as indelicate, of coarse masculine belongings strewn about in endless litter; of dust and disorder arising necessarily from a coarse masculine presence in the midst of all this delicate harmony.

Among her forebodings of disturbance, not the least was with regard to Ceasar. Ceasar was a veritable hermit of a dog. For the greater part of his life he had dwelt in his secluded hut, shut out from the society of his kind and all innocent canine joys. Never had Ceasar since his early youth watched at a woodchuck's hole; never had he known the delights of a stray bone at a neighbor's kitchen door. And it was all on account of a sin committed when hardly out of his puppyhood. No one knew the possible depth of remorse of which this mild-visaged, altogether innocent-looking old dog might be capable; but whether or not he had encountered remorse, he had encountered a full measure of righteous retribution. Old Ceasar seldom lifted up his voice in a growl or a bark; he was fat and sleepy; there were yellow rings which looked like spectacles around his dim old eyes; but there was a neighbor who bore on his hand the imprint of several of Ceasar's sharp white youthful teeth, and for that he had lived at the end of a chain, all alone in a little hut, for fourteen years. The neighbor, who was choleric and smarting with the pain of his wound, had demanded either Ceasar's death or complete ostracism. So Louisa's brother, to whom the dog had belonged, had built him his little kennel and tied him up. It was now fourteen years since, in a flood of youthful spirits, he had inflicted that memorable bite, and with the exception of short excursions, always at the end of the chain, under the strict guardianship of his master or Louisa, the old dog had remained a close prisoner. It is doubtful if, with his limited ambition, he took much pride in the fact, but it is certain that he was possessed of considerable cheap fame. He was regarded by all the children in the village and by many adults as a very monster of ferocity. St. George's dragon could hardly have surpassed in evil repute Louisa Ellis's old yellow dog. Mothers charged their children with solemn emphasis not to go too near to him, and the children listened and believed greedily, with a fascinated appetite for terror, and ran by Louisa's house stealthily, with many sidelong and backward glances at the terrible dog. If perchance he sounded a hoarse bark, there was a panic. Wayfarers chancing into Louisa's yard eyed him with respect, and inquired if the chain were stout. Ceasar at large might have seemed a very ordinary dog, and excited no comment whatever; chained, his reputation overshadowed him, so that he lost his own proper outlines and looked darkly vague and enormous. Joe Dagget, however, with his good-humored sense and shrewdness, saw him as he was. He strode valiantly up to him and patted him on the head, in spite of Louisa's soft clamor of warning, and even attempted to set him loose. Louisa grew so alarmed that he desisted, but kept announcing his opinion in the matter quite forcibly at intervals. "There ain't a better-natured dog in town," he would say, "and it's down-right cruel to keep him tied up there. Some day I'm going to take him out."

Louisa had very little hope that he would not, one of these days, when their interests and possessions should be more completely fused in one. She pictured to herself Ceasar on the rampage through the quiet and unguarded village. She saw innocent children bleeding in his path. She was herself very fond of the old dog, because he had belonged to her dead brother, and he was always very gentle with her; still she had great faith in his ferocity. She always warned people not to go too near him. She fed him on ascetic fare of corn-mush and cakes, and never fired his dangerous temper with heating and sanguinary diet of flesh and bones. Louisa looked at the old dog munching his simple fare, and thought of her approaching marriage and trembled. Still no anticipation of disorder and confusion in lieu of sweet peace and harmony, no forebodings of Ceasar on the rampage, no wild fluttering of her little yellow canary, were sufficient to turn her a hair's breadth. Joe Dagget had been fond of her and working for her all these years. It was not for her, whatever came to pass, to prove untrue and break his heart. She put the exquisite little stitches into her wedding-garments, and the time went on until it was only a week before her wedding-day. It was a Tuesday evening, and the wedding was to be a week from Wednesday.

There was a full moon that night. About nine o'clock Louisa strolled down the road a little way. There were harvest-fields on either hand, bordered by low stone walls. Luxuriant clumps of bushes grew beside the wall, and trees — wild cherry and old apple-trees — at intervals. Presently Louisa sat down on the wall and looked about her with mildly sorrowful reflectiveness. Tall shrubs of blueberry and meadow-sweet, all woven together and tangled with blackberry vines and horsebriers, shut her in on either side. She had a little clear space between them. Opposite her, on the other side of the road, was a spreading tree; the moon shone between its boughs, and the leaves twinkled like silver. The road was bespread with a beautiful shifting dapple of silver and shadow; the air was full of a mysterious sweetness. "I wonder if it's wild grapes?" murmured Louisa. She sat there some time. She was just thinking of rising, when she heard footsteps and low voices, and remained quiet. It was a lonely place, and she felt a little timid. She thought she would keep still in the shadow and let the persons, whoever they might be, pass her.

But just before they reached her the voices ceased, and the footsteps. She understood that their owners had also found seats upon the stone wall. She was wondering if she could not steal away unobserved, when the voice broke the stillness. It was Joe Dagget's. She sat still and listened.

The voice was announced by a loud sigh, which was as familiar as itself. "Well," said Dagget, "you've made up your mind, then, I suppose?"

"Yes," returned another voice, "I'm going day after to-morrow."

"That's Lily Dyer," thought Louisa to herself. The voice embodied itself in her mind. She saw a girl tall and full-figured, with a firm, fair face, looking fairer and firmer in the moonlight, her strong yellow hair braided in a close knot. A girl full of a calm rustic strength and bloom, with a masterful way which might have beseemed a princess. Lily Dyer was a favorite with the village folk; she had just the qualities to arouse the admiration. She was good and handsome and smart. Louisa had often heard her praises sounded.

"Well," said Joe Dagget, "I ain't got a word to say."

"I don't know what you could say," returned Lily Dyer.

"Not a word to say," repeated Joe, drawing out the words heavily. Then there was a silence. "I ain't sorry," he began at last, "that that happened yesterday — that we kind of let on how we felt to each other. I guess it's just as well we knew. Of course I can't do anything any different. I'm going

right on an' get married next week. I ain't going back
on a woman that's waited for me fourteen years, an'
break her heart."

"If you should jilt her to-morrow, I wouldn't have
you," spoke up the girl, with sudden vehemence.

"Well, I ain't going to give you the chance," said
he, "but I don't believe you would, either."

"You'd see I wouldn't. Honor's honor, an' right's
right. An' I'd never think anything of any man that
went against 'em for me or any other girl; you'd find
that out, Joe Dagget."

"Well, you'll find out fast enough that I ain't
going against 'em for you or any other girl," returned
he. Their voices sounded almost as if they were
angry with each other. Louisa was listening eagerly.

"I'm sorry you feel as if you must go away," said
Joe, "but I don't know but it's best."

"Of course it's best. I hope you and I have got
common-sense."

"Well, I suppose you're right." Suddenly Joe's
voice got an undertone of tenderness. "Say, Lily,"

said he, "I'll get along well enough myself, but I can't bear to think — You don't suppose you're going to fret much over it?"

"I guess you'll find out I shan't fret much over a married man."

"Well, I hope you won't — I hope you won't, Lily. God knows I do. And — I hope — one of these days — you'll — come across somebody else —"

"I don't see any reason why I shouldn't." Suddenly her tone changed. She spoke in a sweet, clear voice, so loud that she could have been heard across the street. "No, Joe Dagget," said she, "I'll never marry any other man as long as I live. I've got good sense, an' I ain't going to break my heart nor make a fool of myself; but I'm never going to be married, you can be sure of that. I ain't that sort of a girl to feel this way twice."

Louisa heard an exclamation and a soft commotion behind the bushes; then Lily spoke again — the voice sounded as if she had risen. "This must be put a stop to," said she. "We've stayed here long enough. I'm going home."

Louisa sat there in a daze, listening to their retreating steps. After a while she got up and slunk softly home herself. The next day she did her housework methodically; that was as much a matter of course as breathing; but she did not sew on her wedding-clothes. She sat at her window and meditated. In the evening Joe came. Louisa Ellis had never known that she had any diplomacy in her, but when she came to look for it that night she found it, although meek of its kind, among her little feminine weapons. Even now she could hardly believe that she had heard aright, and that she would not do Joe a terrible injury should she break her troth-plight. She wanted to sound him without betraying too soon her own inclinations in the matter. She did it successfully, and they finally came to an understanding; but it was a difficult thing, for he was as afraid of betraying himself as she.

She never mentioned Lily Dyer. She simply said that while she had no cause of complaint against him, she had lived so long in one way that she shrank from making a change.

"Well, I never shrank, Louisa," said Dagget. "I'm going to be honest enough to say that I think maybe it's better this way; but if you'd wanted to keep on, I'd have stuck to you till my dying day. I hope you know that."

"Yes, I do," said she.

That night she and Joe parted more tenderly than they had done for a long time. Standing in the door, holding each other's hands, a last great wave of regretful memory swept over them.

"Well, this ain't the way we've thought it was all going to end, is it, Louisa?" said Joe.

She shook her head. There was a little quiver on her placid face.

"You let me know if there's ever anything I can do for you," said he, "I ain't ever going to forget you, Louisa." Then he kissed her, and went down the path.

Louisa, all alone by herself that night, wept a

little, she hardly knew why; but the next morning, on waking, she felt like a queen who, after fearing lest her domain be wrested away from her, sees it firmly insured in her possession.

Now the tall weeds and grasses might cluster around Ceasar's little hermit hut, the snow might fall on its roof year in and year out, but he never would go on a rampage through the unguarded village. Now the little canary might turn itself into a peaceful yellow ball night after night, and have no need to wake and flutter with wild terror against its bars. Louisa could sew linen seams, and distil roses, and dust and polish and fold away in lavender, as long as she listed. That afternoon she sat with her needle-work at the window, and felt fairly steeped in peace. Lily Dyer, tall and erect and blooming, went past; but she felt no qualm. If Louisa Ellis had sold her birthright she did not know it, the taste of the pottage was so delicious, and had been her sole satisfaction for so long. Serenity and placid narrowness had become to her as the birthright itself. She gazed ahead through a long reach of future days strung together like pearls in a rosary, every one like the others, and all smooth and flawless and innocent, and her heart went up in thankfulness. Outside was the fervid summer afternoon; the air was filled with the sounds of the busy harvest of men and birds and bees; there were halloos, metallic clatterings, sweet calls, and long hummings. Louisa sat, prayerfully numbering her days, like an uncloistered nun.

# 一女侍

**[爱尔兰] G. 摩尔**

　　觉得自家是再也不会回司各脱兰来了，司替文生在他的小说 *Catriona* 的序文上说："同梦境似的我看见我父亲的幼时，我父亲的父亲（祖父）的幼时，我也看见在那极北一角的生命的源流一直下来，还带着些歌泣的声音，最后轮流到我就同山洪暴发似的将我奔流远送到这极边的岛国里来了。运命的拨弄使我不得不赞美，不得不俯首。"这一句话，岂不是像在一种热情奔放的时候写的，仿佛是一边在写，一边他还在那里追逐幻影的样子，你说是也不是？并且这一句话还可以使我们联想到扑火的灯蛾身上去。总之，不管它的真意如何，这一句话，实在包含着几句很美丽的句子，虽则我们不能照原形将它记着，但总是可以使人念念不忘的。我们即使忘记了"歌

泣"两字和"奔流远送"等字眼，但在我们的记
忆里，却马上有一个比较单纯的字眼来代替的。
司替文生所表现的情感，只在"运命的拨弄""极
边的岛国"等字上迸发出来。世人谁不觉得命运
是拨弄人的？又谁不赞美那运命迁他出去的极边
的岛国？教皇命令出来，要活剥皮的琪亚可莫圣
洗，大约也一定在赞美运命拨弄他的那极边的岛
国，就是行刑者用以将他的大腹皮同前裾似的卷
起来的那块绑缚的板。有一次，我在大街上看见
一只野兔在架上打鼓，它很有意思地望着我，我
晓得这野兔也一定虽则和人不同地在赞美它的
运命，将它从树林里迁徙出来，迁它到提架的上
面，这提架就是它的极边的岛国。但是这两宗运
命的拨弄，并不算稀奇，并没有我遇见的一位爱
尔兰的女孩子的运命那么稀奇。她系在拉丁区的
一家极边的咖啡馆里侍候学生们的饮食的。她当
然也在赞美运命，将她抛将出来，命定她在烟酒
中送她的残生，侍候许多学生，他们爱听什么
话，她就也不得不依顺他们。

在听完戏后，想寻些短时间的娱乐，艾儿
佛、达伐利小姐和我三人，（有一天晚上）终于

闯进了这一家咖啡馆。我本来想，这一个地方，
对于达伐利小姐有点不大适宜，但是艾儿佛说，
我们可以找一个清静的角落去坐的，所以结果就
找到了一个由一位瘦弱的女侍者所招呼的地方。
这一位女招待的厌倦的容颜，幽雅的风度和瘦弱
的体格，竟唤起了我的无限的同情。她的双颊瘦
削，眼色灰蓝，望去略带些忧郁，像 Rosetti 的
画里的神情。波动的紫发，斜覆在额旁耳上也是
洛赛蒂式的很低的环结在脖子的后面。我注意到
了这两位妇人的互相凝视，一个康健多财，一个
贫贱多病。我更猜度到了这两妇人在脑里所惹起
的深思。我想两人一定各在奇异，何以一样的人
生，两人间会有这样的差别？但是在此地我不得
不先说一说谁是达伐利小姐，和我何以会和她认
识。我有一次到罗雪泥曾在吃饭过的泰埠街角的
咖啡馆托儿托尼去。托儿托尼从前是很有名的，
因为据说音乐家的罗雪泥得到两万块钱一年的收
入的时候，他曾说过："现在我对音乐也可以满
足了，总算是得到报酬了，以后我可以每天到托
儿托尼去吃饭去。"就是现在，托儿托尼，也还
是文学家艺术家的聚会之所，这些文人艺士大约

在五点钟的时候，都会到来的，我到巴黎的那一天所以也一直地进了这托儿托尼。到那儿去露一露脸，就可以使大家知道，我是在巴黎了。托儿托尼简直是一种变相的公布所。是在托儿托尼，我就于那一天遇见了一位青年。我的一位老朋友，是一位天才画家，他有一张画在鲁克散蒲儿古陈列着，巴黎的女子大抵都喜欢他的。这一位青年，就是艾儿佛，他拉住了我的手，很起劲地对我说"我正在找你"，他说他听见了我的到来，所以从妈特兰起到托儿托尼止，差不多几家咖啡馆都找遍了。

他所以要找我，就是因为他想找我去和达伐利小姐一道吃饭，我们先要上加飘新街去接她。我把这街名写出来，并不因为是她所住的街和我的小说有关，却因为这名字是一种唤起记忆的材料。喜欢巴黎的人，总喜欢听巴黎的街名，因为街名和粉饰的墙上紧靠着的扶梯、古铜色的前门、叫门的铃索等，是唤起巴黎生活的记忆的线索，并且达伐利小姐自身，就是一个忘不了的好纪念，因为她是皇家剧场的一位女优。我的朋友，也是一个使人不能忘记的怪物，因为他

也是一个以不花钱逛女人为名誉的游荡子，他的
主义是"工作完后，她若喜欢到我的画室里来玩
玩，那我们落得在一道快乐快乐"。但是不管他
的主义是如何的不愿为妇人花钱，而当我在达伐
利小姐的室内看她的装饰品的时候，和当她出来
见我们的时候，他的那种郑重声明，我想是可以
不必的。她的起坐室里，装饰着些十六世纪的铜
物，掘雷斯顿的人形，上面有银的装饰的橱棚，
三张蒲奢的画——代表蒲奢的法国，比利时，
意大利三时代的作风的三张画。当我看了这些装
饰品，正在赞赏的时候，他却郑重地申明说，这
些并不是他送她的，她出来见我们的时候，他又
郑重地申明说，她手上的手钏，也并不是他送她
的，他的这一种申明，我觉得是多事。我觉得特
别提起他的不送她东西这些话来，或者是一种不
大高尚的趣味，因为他的说话，曾使她感到了不
快，并且实际上我也看出了她同他一道出去吃
饭，似乎并不同平常一样十分欢喜似的。

　　我们在发耀馆吃的饭，是一家旧式的菜馆，
那些墙上粉饰成金白色，电灯乐队之类的流行趣
味，却是很少的。饭后就到间壁的奥迪安剧场去

看了一出戏，是一出牧童们在田野里溪流的边上
聚首谈心后，又为了不贞节的女人，互相杀戮的
戏。戏中也有葡萄收获，行列歌唱，田野里的马
车歌唱等种种的场面，可是我们并不觉得有趣。
并且在中幕奏乐的当儿，艾儿佛跑到剧场内的各
处去看朋友去了，将达伐利小姐推给了我。我却
最喜欢看一对恋爱者正在进行中的玩意儿，爱在
这一对恋爱者所坐的恋爱窝巢的边上走走。戏散
了之后，他说："去喝一杯罢！"我们所以就到
了那家学生们常进出的咖啡馆。是一家有挂锦装
饰在壁间窗上，有奥克木桌子摆着，有旧式的酒
杯有穿古式的衣裳的女招待的咖啡馆。是一家时
时有一个学生进来，口衔一个大杯，一吞就尽，
跌来倒去的立起来不笑一脸就走的咖啡馆。达伐
利小姐的美貌和时装，一时把聚在那里的学生们
的野眼吸收尽了。她穿一件织花的衣裳，大帽子
底下，露着她的黑发。她的南方美人特有的丰艳
的肤色在项背上头发稀少的地方，带着一种浅黄
深绿的颜色。两只肩膀，又是很丰肥地在胸挂里
斜驰下去，隐隐在暗示她胸前腰际的线条。将她
的丰满完熟的美和那个女招待的苍白衰弱的美比

较起来，觉得很有趣味。达伐利小姐将扇子斜障在胸前，两唇微启，使一排细小的牙齿，在朱红的嘴唇里露着，高坐在那里。那女招待坐在边上，将两只纤细的手臂支住桌沿，很优美地在参加谈话，只有像电光似的目光一闪射的中间，流露出羡怨的意来，仿佛在说她自己是女人中的一个大失败，而达伐利小姐是一个大成功。她说话的口音，初听还不觉得什么，然而细听一会，却听得出一种不晓是哪一处的口音来。有一处我听出了一个南方的口音，后来又听出了一个北方的，最后我明明白白听到了一句英国的腔调，所以就问她说：

"你倒好像是英国人。"

"我是爱尔兰人，是杜勃林人。"

想到了一个在杜勃林礼教中养大的女孩，受了运命的拨弄，被迁到了这一个极边的咖啡馆里，我就问她，何以会弄到此地来的？她就告诉我说，她离开杜勃林的时候，还只有十六岁，六年前她是到巴黎来做一家人家的家庭教师的。她老和小孩子们到鲁克散蒲儿古公园去玩，并且对他们说的是英国话。有一天有一个学生和她在同一张椅子坐在她的边上。其余的事情，可以不必说而容易地想得出了。但是他没有钱养她，所以她不得不到这一家咖啡馆来做工过活。

"这是和我不相合的职业，但是我有什么法子呢？我们生在世上，不吃究竟不行，而此地的烟气很重，老要使我咳嗽。"

我呆看了她一忽儿，她大约是猜破了我脑里所想的事情了，就告诉我说，她的肺，已经有一边烂去了。我们就又讲到了养生，讲到了南方的天地。她又说，医生却劝她到南方去养病去。

艾儿佛和达伐利小姐讲话正在讲得起劲，所以我就靠向了前把注意力的全部都注在这一个可怜的爱尔兰女孩子的身上。她的痨症，她的古式的红裙，她的在皱褶很多的长袖口露着的纤纤的手臂，却引起了我的无穷的兴味。照咖啡馆里的惯例，我不得不请她喝酒的。但她说，酒是于她的身体有害的，可是不喝又不好，或者我可以请她吃一碟牛排。我答应了请，她叫了一碟生牛排，我但须将眼睛一闭，而让她走上屋角去切一块生牛肉下来藏着。她说她想在睡觉之前再吃，睡觉总须在两个钟头以后，大约是午前三点钟的时候。我一边和她说话，一边却在空想南方的一间草舍，在橄榄与橘子树的中间，一个充满着花香的明窗，而坐在窗畔息着的，却是这个少女。

"我倒很喜欢带你到南方去，去看养你的病。"

"我怕你就要讨厌起来。并且你对我的好意，我也不能相当地报答你，医生说，我已经不能再爱什么人了。"

大约我们是已经谈得很久了，因为艾儿佛和达伐利小姐立起来要去的时候，我仿佛是从梦里惊醒过来的样子。艾儿佛见了我那一种样子，就笑着对达伐利小姐说，把我留在咖啡馆里，和新相识的女朋友在一道，倒是一件好事。他的取笑的话插穿了，我虽则很想剩在咖啡馆里，但也不得不跟他们走到街上去。皎洁的月光，照在街上，照在鲁克散蒲儿古的公园里。我在前头已经说过，我最喜欢看一对恋爱者正在进行中的玩意儿，可是深夜人静，一个人在马路上跑，却也有点悲哀。我并不再向那咖啡馆跑，我只一个人在马路上行行走去，心里尽在想刚才的那个女孩子，一边又在想她的一定不可避免的死，因为在那个咖啡馆里，她一定是活不久长的。在月光的底下。

　　在半夜里，这时候城市已经变成了黑色的雕刻了，我们都不得不想来想去地想，我们若看看卷旋的河水，诗意自然会冲上心来。那一天晚上，不但诗意冲上了我的心头，到了新桥附近，文字却自然地联结起来，歌咏起来了，我就于上床之先，写下了开头的几行，第二天早晨，继续做了下去，差不多一天的光阴，都为这一首小诗所费了。

> 只有我和您！我且把爱你的原因讲给
> 　你听，
> 何以你那倦怠的容颜，琴样的声音，
> 对于我会如此的可爱，如此的芳醇，
> 我的爱您，心诚意诚，浑不是一般世俗
> 　的恋情。
> 他们的爱你，不过是为你那灰色的柔和
> 　的眼睛，
> 你那风姿婀娜，亭亭玉立的长身。
> 或者是为了别种痴念，别种邪心，

但我的爱你，却并非是为这种原因。

你且听，听，

我要把爱你的原因讲给你听。

我爱看夕阳残照的风情，

我爱看衰飒绝人的运命，

夕阳下去，天上只留存一味悲哀的寂静，

那一种静色，似在唱哀婉的歌声，

低音慢节，一词一句，总觉伤神，

可怜如此，你那生命，也就要消停，

绝似昙花一现，阴气森森，

你的死去，仿佛是夕阳下坠，天上的柔

　　和暮色，渐减空明，……

我要把你死前的时间留定，

我的爱正值得此种酬报，我敢声明。

我虽则不曾爱过任何人，

但我今番爱你，却是出于至诚的心。

我明知道为时短促，是不长久的柔情，

这柔情的结果，便是无限的凄清，

而这凄清的苦味，却能把浓欢肉欲，化

　　洁扬尘，

因为死神的双臂，已向你而伸，

他要求你去，去做他的夫人。

或者我的痴心，不可以以爱情来命名。

但眼看你如春花的谢去，如逸思的飞升，

却能使我，感觉到一种异样的欢欣，

比较些常人的情感，只觉得纯真。

你且听，听，

我要拣一个麦田千里的乡村，

在那里金黄的麦穗，远接天际的浮云，

平原内或许有小山几处，几条树荫下的
　　野路纵横，

我将求这样的一处村落，去度我俩的蜜
　　月良辰；

去租一间草舍，回廊上，窗门口，要长
　　满着牵缠的青藤，

看出去，要有个宽大的庭园。绿叶重荫，

在园里，我们俩，可以闲步尽新秋残夏
　　的黄昏，

两人的步伐，渐渐短缩，一步一步，渐
　　　走渐轻，

看那橙花树底，庭园的尽处，似乎远不
　　可行，

你将时时歇着，将你的衰容倦貌，靠上
　我的胸襟，

再过片刻，你的倦体消停，

我就不得不将你抱起抱向那有沙发放着
　的窗棂，

在那里你可吸尽黄昏的空气，空气里有
　花气氤氲。

最可怜，是我此时情。

看了你这般神色，便不觉百感横生。

像一天阴闷的天色，到晚来倍觉动人，

增加了那种沉静的颜色，蓦然间便来了
　夜色阴森，

如此幽幽寂寂，你将柔和地睡去，我便
　和你永不得再相亲。

我将悲啼日夜，颗颗大泪，流成你脸上
　的斑纹，

将你放向红薇帐底，我可向幻想里飞腾，

沉思默想，我可做许多吊莫你的诗文。

我更可想到，你已离去红尘，

你已离去了一切卑污的欲念，正像那颗
　天上的明星，

　　她已向暮天深处，隐隐西沉。

　　死是终无所苦，唉，唉，我且更要感谢
　　　死的恩神，

　　因为他给了我洁白的礼品，与深远的
　　　和平，

　　这些事在凡人尘世，到哪里去追寻。

　　这当然不是整个的好诗，但却是几行很好的
长句，每行都是费过推敲的句子，只有末尾倒数
的第二句差了些，文中的省略，是不大好的，光
省去一个"与"字，也不见得会十分出色。

　　死是终无所苦，我要对死神感谢深恩，

　　感谢他给我了一个洁白的不求酬报的爱
　　　情的礼品。

　　哼哼地念着末数行的诗，我一边就急跑到鲁
克散蒲儿古公园附近的那家咖啡馆去。心里却在
寻想，我究竟有这样的勇气没有？去要求她和我
一道上南方去住。或者是没有这样的勇气的，因
为使我这样兴奋的，只是一种幻想，并不是那种

事实。诗人的灵魂，却不是慈善家那丁艾儿的灵魂。我的确是在为她担忧，我所以急急地走往她那里去，我也不能说出为的是什么。当然不是将那首诗去献给她看，这事情的轻轻一念也是肉麻得不可耐的事情。在路上我也停住了好几次，问我自家为什么要去，去有什么事情？可是不待我自己的回答，两只脚却向前跑了，不过心里却混然感觉到，原因是存在我自己的心里的。我想试试看，究竟我是能不能为他人牺牲一切的，所以进了咖啡馆，找了是她招待的一张桌子上坐下的时候，我就在等。但是等了半天，她却不来，我就问边上的一位学生，问他可晓得那个女招待。他说他晓得的，并且告诉了我她的病状。他说她是没有希望的了，只有血清注射的一法，还可以救她的命，她是已经差不多没有血液在身上了。他详细地述说如何可以从一个康健的人的手臂上取出血清来，如何注射到无血的人的脉里去。不过他在说着，我觉得周围的物影朦胧起来了，而他的声气也渐渐地微弱了下去。我忽而听见一个人说：“喂，你脸上青得很！”并且听见他为我要了白兰地来。南方的空气，大约是疗她不好的，实际上是无法可施了，所以我终于空自想着她的样子而跑回了家里。

二十年过去了。我又想起了她。这可怜的爱尔兰的姑娘！被运命同急流似的抛了出去，抛到了那一家极边的咖啡馆里。这一堆可怜的白骨！我也不觉对运命俯了首，赞美着它，因为运命的奇迹，使我这只见过她一面的人，倒成了一个最后的纪念她的人。不过我若当时不写那首诗或者我也已经将她忘了。这一首诗，我现在想奉献给她，做一个她的无名的纪念。

\* \* \* \* \* \*

本文系自 George Moore's *Memoirs of My Dead Life* 里译出，题名 *A Waitress*，原书是美国 D.Appleton & Co.1932年版。

一九一七年九月十九日

# A Waitress

## by George Moore

*F*eeling that he would never see Scotland again, Stevenson wrote in a preface to "Catriona":—"I see like a vision the youth of my father, and of his father, and the whole stream of lives flowing down there far in the north, with the sound of laughter and tears, to cast me out in the end, as by a sudden freshet, on these ultimate islands. And I admire and bow my head before the romance of destiny." Does not this sentence read as if it were written in stress of some effusive febrile emotion, as if he wrote while still pursuing his idea? And so it reminds us of a moth fluttering after a light. But however vacillating, the sentence contains some pretty clauses, and it will be remembered though not perhaps in its original form. We shall forget the "laughter and the tears" and the "sudden freshet", and a simpler phrase will form itself in our memories. The emotion that Stevenson had to express transpires only in the words, "romance of destiny, ultimate islands." Who does not feel his destiny to be a romance, and who does not admire the ultimate island whither his destiny will cast him? Giacomo Cenci, whom the Pope ordered to be flayed alive, no doubt admired the romance of destiny that laid him on his ultimate island, a raised plank, so that the executioner might conveniently roll up the skin of his belly like an apron. And a hare that I once saw beating a tambourine in Regent Street looked at me so wistfully that I am sure it admired in some remote way the romance of destiny that had taken it from the woodland and cast it upon its ultimate island—in this case a barrow. But neither of these strange examples of the romance of destiny seems to me more wonderful than the destiny of a wistful Irish girl whom I saw serving drinks to students in a certain ultimate café in the Latin Quarter; she, too, no doubt, admired the destiny which had cast her out, ordaining that she should die amid tobacco smoke, serving drinks to students, entertaining them with whatever conversation they desired.

Gervex, Mademoiselle D'Avary, and I had gone to this café after the theatre for half an hour's distraction; I had thought that the place seemed too rough for Mademoiselle D'Avary, but Gervex had said that we should find a quiet corner, and we had happened to choose one in charge of a thin, delicate girl, a girl touched with languor, weakness, and a grace which interested and moved me; her cheeks were thin, and the deep grey eyes were wistful as a drawing of Rossetti; her waving brown hair fell over the temples, and was looped up low over the neck after the Rossetti fashion. I had noticed how the two women looked at each other, one woman healthful and rich, the other poor and ailing; I had guessed the thought that passed across their minds. Each had doubtless asked and wondered why life had come to them so differently. But first I must tell who was Mademoiselle D'Avary, and how I came to know her. I had gone to Tortoni, a once-celebrated café at the corner of the Rue Taitbout, the dining place of Rossini. When Rossini had earned an income of two thousand pounds a year it is recorded that he said, "Now I've done with music, it has served its turn, and I'm going to dine every day at Tortoni's." Even in my time Tortoni was the rendezvous of the world of art and letters; every one was there at five o'clock, and to Tortoni I went the day I arrived in Paris. To be seen there would make known the fact that I was in Paris. Tortoni was a sort of publication. At Tortoni I had discovered a young man, one of my oldest friends, a painter of talent—he had a picture in the Luxembourg—and a man who was beloved by women. Gervex, for it was he, had seized me by the hand, and with voluble eagerness had told me that I was the person he was seeking: he had heard of my coming and had sought me in every café from the Madeleine to Tortoni. He had been seeking

me because he wished to ask me to dinner to meet
Mademoiselle D'Avary; we were to fetch her in the
Rue des Capucines. I write the name of the street, not
because it matters to my little story in what street she
lived, but because the name is an evocation. Those
who like Paris like to hear the names of the streets,
and the long staircase turning closely up the painted
walls, the brown painted doors on the landings,
and the bell rope, are evocative of Parisian life; and
Mademoiselle D'Avary is herself an evocation, for
she was an actress of the Palais Royal. My friend,
too, is an evocation, he was one of those whose pride
is not to spend money upon women, whose theory of
life is that, "If she likes to come round to the studio
when one's work is done, nous pouvons faire la fête
ensemble." But however defensible this view of life
may be, and there is much to be said for it, I had
thought that he might have refrained from saying
when I looked round the drawing-room admiring
it—a drawing-room furnished with sixteenth-century
bronzes, Dresden figures, étagères covered with

silver ornaments, three drawings by Boucher—
Boucher in three periods, a French Boucher, a
Flemish Boucher, and an Italian Boucher—that I
must not think that any of these things were presents
from him, and from saying when she came into the
room that the bracelet on her arm was not from him.
It had seemed to me in slightly bad taste that he
should remind her that he made no presents, for his
remark had clouded her joyousness; I could see that
she was not so happy at the thought of going out to
dine with him as she had been.

It was chez Foyoz that we dined, an old-
fashioned restaurant still free from the new taste
that likes walls painted white and gold, electric
lamps and fiddlers. After dinner we had gone to
see a play next door at the Odéon, a play in which
shepherds spoke to each other about singing brooks,
and stabbed each other for false women, a play
diversified with vintages, processions, wains, and
songs. Nevertheless it had not interested us. And
during the entr'actes Gervex had paid visits in

various parts of the house, leaving Mademoiselle
D'Avary to make herself agreeable to me. I dearly
love to walk by the perambulator in which Love is
wheeling a pair of lovers. After the play he had said,
"Allons boire un bock," and we had turned into a
students' café, a café furnished with tapestries and
oak tables, and old-time jugs and Medicis gowns,
a café in which a student occasionally caught up a
tall bock in his teeth, emptied it at a gulp, and after
turning head over heels, walked out without having
smiled. Mademoiselle D'Avary's beauty and fashion
had drawn the wild eyes of all the students gathered
there. She wore a flower-enwoven dress, and from
under the large hat her hair showed dark as night;
and her southern skin filled with rich tints, yellow
and dark green where the hair grew scanty on the
neck; the shoulders drooped into opulent suggestion
in the lace bodice. And it was interesting to compare
her ripe beauty with the pale deciduous beauty of the
waitress. Mademoiselle D'Avary sat, her fan wide-
spread across her bosom, her lips parted, the small

teeth showing between the red lips. The waitress sat, her thin arms leaning on the table, joining very prettily in the conversation, betraying only in one glance that she knew that she was only a failure and Mademoiselle D'Avary a success. It was some time before the ear caught the slight accent; an accent that was difficult to trace to any country. Once I heard a southern intonation, and then a northern; finally I heard an unmistakable English intonation, and said, "But you're English."

"I'm Irish. I'm from Dublin."

And thinking of a girl reared in its Dublin conventions, but whom the romance of destiny had cast upon this ultimate café, I asked her how she had found her way here; and she told me she had left Dublin when she was sixteen; she had come to Paris six years ago to take a situation as nursery governess. She used to go with the children into the Luxembourg Gardens and talk to them in English. One day a student had sat on the bench beside her. The rest of the story is easily guessed. But he had no money to keep her, and she had to come to this café to earn her living.

"It doesn't suit me, but what am I to do? One must live, and the tobacco smoke makes me cough." I sat looking at her, and she must have guessed what was passing in my mind, for she told me that one lung was gone; and we spoke of health, of the South, and she said that the doctor had advised her to go away south.

Seeing that Gervex and Mademoiselle D'Avary were engaged in conversation, I leaned forward and devoted all my attention to this wistful Irish girl, so interesting in her phthisis, in her red Medicis gown, her thin arms showing in the long rucked sleeves. I had to offer her drink; to do so was the custom of the place. She said that drink harmed her, but she would get into trouble if she refused drink; perhaps I would not mind paying for a piece of beef-steak instead. She had been ordered raw steak! I have only to close my eyes to see her going over to the corner of the café and cutting a piece and putting it away. She said she would eat it before going to bed, and that would be two hours hence, about three. While talking to her I thought of a cottage in the South amid olive and orange trees, an open window full of fragrant air, and this girl sitting by it.

"I should like to take you south and attend upon you."

"I'm afraid you would grow weary of nursing me. And I should be able to give you very little in return for your care. The doctor says I'm not to love any one." We must have talked for some time, for it was like waking out of a dream when Gervex and Mademoiselle D'Avary got up to go, and, seeing how interested I was, he laughed, saying to Mademoiselle D'Avary that it would be kind to leave me with my new friend. His pleasantry jarred, and though I should like to have remained, I followed them into the street, where the moon was shining over the Luxembourg Gardens. And as I have said before, I dearly love to walk by a perambulator in which Love is wheeling a pair of lovers, but it is sad to find oneself alone on the pavement at midnight. Instead of going back to the café I wandered on, thinking of the girl I had seen, and of her certain death, for she could not live many months in that café. We all want to think at midnight, under the moon, when the city looks like a black Italian engraving, and poems come to us as we watch a swirling river. Not only the idea of a poem came to me that night, but on the Pont Neuf the words began to sing together, and I jotted down the first lines before going to bed. Next morning I continued my poem, and all day was passed in this little composition.

*We are alone! Listen, a little while,*
*And hear the reason why your weary smile*
*And lute-toned speaking are so very sweet,*
*And how my love of you is more complete*
*Than any love of any lover.*
*They have only been attracted by the grey*
*Delicious softness of your eyes, your slim*
*And delicate form, or some such other whim,*

*The simple pretexts of all lovers;—I*

*For other reason. Listen whilst I try*

*To say. I joy to see the sunset slope*

*Beyond the weak hours' hopeless horoscope,*

*Leaving the heavens a melancholy calm*

*Of quiet colour chaunted like a psalm,*

*In mildly modulated phrases; thus*

*Your life shall fade like a voluptuous*

*Vision beyond the sight, and you shall die*

*Like some soft evening's sad serenity....*

*I would possess your dying hours; indeed*

*My love is worthy of the gift, I plead*

*For them. Although I never loved as yet,*

*Methinks that I might love you; I would get*

*From out the knowledge*

*That the time was brief,*

*That tenderness, whose pity grows to grief,*

*And grief that sanctifies, a joy, a charm*

*Beyond all other loves, for now the arm*

*Of Death is stretched to you-ward,*

*And he claims*

*You as his bride. Maybe my soul misnames*

*Its passion; love perhaps it is not, yet*

*To see you fading like a violet,*

*Or some sweet thought,*

*Would be a very strange*

*And costly pleasure, far beyond the range*

*Of formal man's emotion. Listen, I*

*Will chose a country spot where fields of rye*

*And wheat extend in rustling yellow plains,*

*Broken with wooded hills and leafy lanes,*

*To pass our honeymoon; a cottage where*

*The porch and windows are*

*Festooned with fair*

*Green leaves of eglantine, and look upon*

*A shady garden where we'll walk alone*

*In the autumn summer evenings;*

*Each will see*

*Our walks grow shorter,*

*Till to the orange tree,*

*The garden's length, is far, and you will rest*

*From time to time, leaning upon my breast*

*Your languid lily face, then later still*

*Unto the sofa by the window-sill*

*Your wasted body I shall carry, so*

*That you may drink the*

*last left lingering glow*

*Of evening, when the air is filled with scent*

*Of blossoms; and my spirits shall be rent*

*The while with many griefs.*

*Like some blue day*

*That grows more lovely as it fades away,*

*Gaining that calm serenity and height*

*Of colour wanted, as the solemn night*

*Steals forward you will sweetly fall asleep*

*For ever and for ever; I shall weep*

*A day and night large tears upon your face,*

*Laying you then beneath a rose-red place*

*Where I may muse and dedicate and dream*

*Volumes of poesy of you; and deem*

*It happiness to know that you are far*

*From any base desires as that fair star*

*Set in the evening magnitude of heaven.*

*Death takes but little, yea,*

*Your death has given me*

*That deep peace*

*And immaculate possession*

*Which man may never find*

*In earthly passion.*

Good poetry of course not, but good verse, well turned every line except the penultimate. The elision is not a happy one, and the mere suppression of the "and" does not produce a satisfying line.

*Death takes but little,*

*Death I thank for giving*

*Me a remembrance, and a pure possession*

*Of unrequited love.*

And mumbling the last lines of the poem, I hastened to the café near the Luxembourg Gardens, wondering if I should find courage to ask the girl to come away to the South and live, fearing that I should not, fearing it was the idea rather than the deed that tempted me; for the soul of a poet is not the soul of Florence Nightingale. I was sorry for this wistful Irish girl, and was hastening to her, I knew not why; not to show her the poem—the very thought was intolerable. Often did I stop on the way to ask myself why I was going, and on what errand. Without discovering an answer in my heart I hastened on, feeling, I suppose, in some blind way that my quest was in my own heart. I would know if it were capable of making a sacrifice; and sitting down at one of her tables I waited, but she did not come, and I asked the student by me if he knew the girl generally in charge of these tables. He said he did, and told me about her case. There was no hope for her; only a transfusion of blood could save her; she was almost bloodless. He described how blood could be taken from the arm of a healthy man and passed into the veins of the almost bloodless. But as he spoke things began to get dim and his voice to grow faint; I heard some one saying, "You're very pale," and he ordered some brandy for me. The South could not save her; practically nothing could; and I returned home thinking of her.

Twenty years have passed, and I am thinking of her again. Poor little Irish girl! Cast out in the end by a sudden freshet on an ultimate café. Poor little heap of bones! And I bow my head and admire the romance of destiny which ordained that I, who only saw her once, should be the last to remember her. Perhaps I should have forgotten her had it not been that I wrote a poem, a poem which I now inscribe and dedicate to her nameless memory.